Discovering Connecticut: Your Essential First-Time Travel Guide

Jemima .Y Shaw

All rights reserved. Copyright © 2023 Jemima .Y Shaw

Funny helpful tips:

Practice gratitude daily; it shifts your focus from what's lacking to what's abundant.

Stay proactive in seeking out diverse authors; their unique experiences enrich the literary landscape.

Discovering Connecticut: Your Essential First-Time Travel Guide : Explore the Best of Connecticut: An Unforgettable Travel Experience for First-Time Tourists

Life advices:

Practice mindfulness; it anchors you to the present and reduces stress.

Engage in regular financial forecasting; it aids in planning and strategy.

Introduction

This book serves as a comprehensive guide to discovering the unique and offbeat attractions in Connecticut. The guide begins with an introduction to Connecticut's landscape and climate, setting the stage for an exploration of its diverse destinations.

From cultural landmarks like the Wadsworth Atheneum, Elizabeth Park, and the Connecticut Historical Society to the natural beauty of places like Bigelow Hollow State Park, Talcott Mountain, and Enders Falls, the guide covers a wide range of attractions. Readers are introduced to various parks, trails, and scenic spots, including Nipmuck State Forest, Ragged Mountain, Saville Dam, and more.

The guide takes a detailed look at key destinations such as Litchfield Hills, Burr Pond State Park, Kent Falls State Park, and the Appalachian Trail. It provides insights into lesser-known gems like Tory's Cave, Riga Falls, and the Montgomery Pinetum.

Readers are invited to explore the vibrant cultural scene with visits to museums and historic sites like The Aldrich Contemporary Art Museum, Philip Johnson Glass House, and Keeler Tavern Museum. The culinary scene is also highlighted with mentions of popular markets like Fjord Fish Market and events like the Westport Farmers' Market.

The coastal beauty of Connecticut is showcased through destinations like Sherwood Island State Park, Silver Sands State Park, and the Thimble Islands. The guide doesn't neglect urban attractions, featuring spots such as the Palace Theatre, Yale University, and the Ely Center of Contemporary Art in New Haven.

Practical considerations are addressed in the final section, emphasizing the importance of proper planning for an enjoyable exploration of Connecticut's diverse and offbeat destinations. Overall, this guide is a valuable resource for both residents and visitors looking to uncover the hidden gems and must-visit places in Connecticut.

Contents

About Connecticut 1
Landscape and Climate 3
Wadsworth Atheneum 5
Elizabeth Park 6
Charter Oak Landing 7
Connecticut Historical Society 8
Connecticut Science Center 9
Connecticut State Capitol 10
The Mark Twain House & Museum 11
Old State House 12
The Bushnell Performing Arts Center 13
Harriet Beecher Stowe Center 14
Mortensen Riverfront Plaza 15
Museum of Connecticut History 16
Bushnell Park 17
Nipmuck State Forest 18
Bigelow Hollow State Park 19
Metacomet 20
Talcott Mountain 21
Ragged Mountain 22
Enders State Forest 23
Enders Falls 24
Saville Dam 25
Farmington River 26

National Iwo Jima Memorial	27
Tunxis Trail	28
Litchfield Hills	29
Burr Pond State Park	30
Campbell Falls State Park	31
Steep Rock Preserve	32
Yellow Circle Blazes Loop	33
Lake Waramaug	34
Bantam Lake	35
Mattatuck Trail	36
Riga Falls	37
Bear Mountain Trail	38
Mount Frissell	39
Cathedral Pines	40
Kent Falls State Park	41
Macedonia Brook State Park	42
Appalachian Trail	43
Tory's Cave	44
The Aldrich Contemporary Art Museum	45
Keeler Tavern Museum and History Center	46
Philip Johnson Glass House	47
Diane's Books	48
Fjord Fish Market	49
Flinn Gallery	50
Greenwich Avenue Historic District	51
Greenwich Point Park	52
Putnam Cottage	53

Montgomery Pinetum	54
Greenwich Audubon Center	55
Bruce Park	56
Bush-Holley House	57
Cove Island Park	58
Cummings Park	59
First Presbyterian Church	60
Half Full Brewery	61
Fort Stamford Park	62
Stamford Museum & Nature Center	63
Stamford Observatory	64
The Ferguson Library	65
Mianus River Park	66
Mill River Park	67
Bartlett Arboretum & Gardens	68
Earthplace	69
Compo Beach	70
Westport Country Playhouse	71
Westport Farmers' Market	72
Westport Museum for History and Culture	73
Westport Paddle Club	74
Levitt Pavilion for the Performing Arts	75
Longshore Park	76
MoCA Westport	77
Sherwood Island State Park	78
Lake Mohegan	79
Trout Brook Valley State Park	80

Twin Brooks Park	81
Indian Well State Park	82
Palace Theatre	83
Mirror Lake	84
Chauncey Peak Trail	85
Mattabesett Blue Trail	86
Sleeping Giant State Park	87
Silver Sands State Park	88
Charles Island	89
East Rock Park	90
Ely Center of Contemporary Art	91
Carousel at Lighthouse Point Park	92
Yale Peabody Museum of Natural History	93
Yale University	94
New Haven Green	94
Kehler Liddell Gallery	96
The Blessed Michael McGivney Pilgrimage Center	97
Beinecke Rare Book & Manuscript Library	98
Shore Line Trolley Museum	99
Thimble Islands	100
Audubon Guilford Salt Meadow Sanctuary	101
Hammonasset State Park	102
West Beach	103
Harvey's Beach	104
General William Hart House	105
The Preserve	106
Katharine Hepburn Cultural Arts Center	107

Lynde Point Lighthouse	108
Connecticut River	109
White Sands Beach	110
Florence Griswold Museum	111
The Robert and Nancy Krieble Gallery	112
Rocky Neck State Park	113
Ocean Beach Park	114
Bluff Point State Park	115
Mystic River and Village	116
Hopeville Pond	117
Millers Pond	118
Devil's Hopyard State Park	119
Cockaponset State Forest	120
Gillette Castle Park	121
Goodspeed Opera House	122
Wadsworth Falls State Park	123
Dinosaur State Park	124
Proper Planning	125

About Connecticut

A small state located on the east coast, Connecticut is officially nicknamed "The Constitution State." It is thought to be the first territory or colony to have adopted a form of constitution with its Fundamental Orders in the year 1639. It entered into statehood with the U.S. in 1788, becoming the fifth state.

Connecticut was named after the Native American word *quinatucquet*, which translates to "beside the long tidal river." The Native Americans gave this area that name because of the Connecticut River, which splits the state in half. Native American tribes that called this area home include the Pequot, Mohegan, and Niantic tribes.

Dutch traders arrived in Connecticut in 1614 and established the first European settlement in the New World in 1633. English settlers also claimed land in the area, and the territory became a British colony in the latter part of the 17th century. Connecticut was centrally featured during the American Revolution, and in 1776, its representatives signed the Declaration of Independence.

Hartford has been the capitol since its inception in 1875. It is centrally located in the state, making it a convenient starting point for many state adventures. Several famous inventors have called Connecticut home, including Elias Howe, Eli Whitney, Charles Goodyear, Edwin H. Land, and Eli Terry. It is well-known for inventions like typewriters and watches.

Connecticut has eight counties that encompass 109 state parks, which is a relatively high number considering the state's overall size. It's a favorite resort destination, with 250 miles of shoreline on the Long Island Sound and numerous inland lakes. It is also renowned for being the home of Yale University and various major museums, including the Gallery of Fine Arts, Peabody Museum, Winchester Gun Museum, P.T. Barnum Museum, and the American Clock and Watch Museum.

Landscape and Climate

The state is divided into three geographic regions, which are known as the Western Upland, the Central Lowland, and the Eastern Upland. It is bordered by Rhode Island to the east, New York to the west, Massachusetts to the north, and the Long Island Sound to the south.

The Western Upland covers approximately a third of the state and is characterized by steep hills, including Mount Frissell, the highest point in Connecticut. Volcanic eruptions created the valleys and ridges that make up the Central Lowlands in the middle of the state, and igneous rocks are still prominent in this area. In the Eastern Upland, you'll find dense forests, rolling hills, and rushing rivers.

Almost two-thirds of Connecticut is covered in forests, which produce the state's top natural resource: wood. These forests are responsible for Connecticut's lumber, maple syrup, and firewood industries. Of the myriad trees you'll find in the state, the most common are red maple, sugar maple, eastern hemlock, and black birch.

Along the southern border, the climate is hot and humid during the summer, and cool and rainy during the winter. Snow is infrequent in this area, as it is the transition zone between the south and north. In the northern part of the state, snow is much more common during the winter and averages about 60 inches each year. There are usually fewer than 60 days of snow per year, and the state averages 56% of possible sunshine annually, which is higher than the national average.

Spring is normally cool with highs in the 60s and 70s, but by late May, the south begins to get humid and hot while the north remains temperate. Connecticut is a popular locale for visitors who want to see the fall foliage because of all the trees in the state. Plus, the mild autumn temperatures allow the leaves to change color gradually before falling off the trees in November.

Wadsworth Atheneum

Wadsworth Atheneum is the nation's oldest free public museum, and it features over 50,000 works of art. The Gothic-style structure dates back to 1842, when Daniel Wadsworth, an early American art patron, founded the museum to showcase works of art, artifacts, and literature. Originally, it was planned to be solely a gallery of fine arts, but Wadsworth changed directions and instead established an atheneum, which refers to a cultural institution. Highlights of work at the facility include artwork by Salvador Dalí and Caravaggio, the Wallace Nutting Collection of Early American Furniture, and more.

Best Time to Visit: The Wadsworth Atheneum is open on Friday from 12:00 p.m. to 8:00 p.m., and Saturday and Sunday from 12:00 p.m. to 5:00 p.m. all year.

Pass/Permit/Fees: Adult admission is $15; seniors are $12; college students are $5; and youth under the age of 18 are free.

Closest City or Town: Hartford, Connecticut

How to Get There: From New Haven: Take I-91 north for 36.7 miles to Whitehead Highway in Hartford. Take Exit 29A onto Whitehead Highway. Travel for 0.5 miles to Prospect Street, and take Prospect Street to Atheneum Square, where the museum is located.

GPS Coordinates: 41.7637° N, -72.6731°W

Did You Know? A major $33 million renovation to the museum in 2015 paved the way for 17 new galleries to allow patrons to see more art and artifacts during a single visit.

Elizabeth Park

Elizabeth Park offers visitors more than 100 acres of gardens, recreational facilities, green space, and hiking paths. It also hosts various special activities like concerts, workshops, and lectures. When the gardens are in full bloom, the park is a treasure trove of photo opportunities for photographers of all levels. The Helen S. Kaman Rose Garden is the first municipal rose garden in the U.S. and is currently the third-largest rose garden in the nation. Other incredible gardens in this park include the Charlie Ortiz Hosta Garden, the Julian and Edith Eddy Rock Garden, and the Robert A. Prill Tulip Garden.

Best Time to Visit: Most gardens are in full bloom between June and September, so the best time to visit is during those months.

Pass/Permit/Fees: There is no fee to visit Elizabeth Park.

Closest City or Town: West Hartford, Connecticut

How to Get There: From the north or south: Take I-91 either north or south to I-84 W toward Waterbury. From I-84, take Exit 48 onto Asylum Avenue. Travel for 1.9 miles to Prospect Avenue. Turn left onto Prospect Avenue, go for about 500 feet, and turn right at the park's entrance.

GPS Coordinates: 41.7746° N, -72.7194° W

Did You Know? The Elizabeth Pond Memorial Building, also known as the Pond House, is home to the Pond House Café, which offers everything from snacks to full meals. It was originally a Victorian Mansion that was built in 1870, but it was remodeled in 1959 to become a more modern-styled community center.

Charter Oak Landing

Charter Oak Landing is a park located south of downtown Hartford. It features a public boat launch, an excursion boat dock, and access to the Great River Park via the Charter Oak Bridge pedestrian walkway. Besides being the home of a pair of nesting eagles, Charter Oak Landing also has paved and lighted walkways, picnic tables, a playground, charcoal grills, and fishing areas. This is an ideal location to visit for an afternoon of fishing, barbecuing, or just enjoying nature.

Best Time to Visit: Summer is the best time to visit.

Pass/Permit/Fees: There is no fee to visit.

Closest City or Town: Hartford, Connecticut

How to Get There: From the north or south: Take I-91 to Airport Road at Exit 27. Turn left onto Airport Road, then left onto Brainard Road. Take a final left onto Reserve Road. You'll see the park's entrance on the right.

From the east or west: Take I-84 to Hartford, then take Exit 57 for Charter Oak Bridge. Continue onto US-5/Connecticut Highway 15 South to Exit 87 for Brainard Road. Turn left onto Brainard Road, then left onto Reserve Road. You'll see the park's entrance on the right.

GPS Coordinates: 41.7546° N, -72.6586° W

Did You Know? Striped bass can be caught in the waters off Charter Oak Landing, particularly during late spring when they move upriver chasing after spawning shad and herring. It is not uncommon for anglers to pull 30- to 60-inch fish from this area.

Connecticut Historical Society

The Connecticut Historical Society is a nonprofit organization that was formed in 1825, which makes it one of the oldest in the country. The building is home to a library, museum, and the Edgar F. Waterman Research Center. The main historical collection features over four million documents, books, artifacts, images, and other materials that trace Connecticut's rich history in the U.S. The Connecticut Historical Society's mission is to educate the community on the history and culture of Connecticut, along with its pivotal role in American history.

Best Time to Visit: The museum is open Tuesday through Friday between 12:00 p.m. and 5:00 p.m., and on Saturday from 9:00 a.m. to 5:00 p.m. The library and research center are open Tuesday, Wednesday, Friday, and Saturday from 12:00 p.m. to 2:00 p.m. and 2:30 p.m. to 4:30 p.m., but you must have an appointment.

Pass/Permit/Fees: Adult admission is $12; seniors are $10; and students are $8. Children ages 5 and under are free.

Closest City or Town: Hartford, Connecticut

How to Get There: From I-84 West: Take Exit 46 and turn right onto Sisson Avenue. Turn left onto Farmington Avenue (second traffic light), then right onto Girard Avenue (first right). At the second intersection, turn right onto Elizabeth Street. You'll see the building on the right.

GPS Coordinates: 41.7729° N, -72.7053° W

Did You Know?
Adults can get a guided 45- to 60-minute tour with a reservation. No children will be on the tour.

Connecticut Science Center

Children, teens, and adults will all love the various experiences they will have at the Connecticut Science Center. There are over 165 hands-on exhibits to engage in scientific experimentation in physics, geology, astronomy, forensics, and more. Plus, there is a cutting-edge 3D digital theater and four educational laboratories to explore even more amazing scientific concepts. The breadth of what visitors can learn at the Connecticut Science Center makes it a model for science education nationwide.

Best Time to Visit: Since the center is closed on Monday and Tuesday, the best times to visit are Wednesday through Sunday from 10:00 a.m. to 3:00 p.m. (4:00 p.m. on weekends).

Pass/Permit/Fees: Adult admission is $24.95 per person, and children between the ages of 3 and 17 are $16.95. Children ages 2 and under are free, and seniors ages 65+ are $22.95. The Butterfly Encounter is an additional $5.00 per person.

Closest City or Town: Hartford, Connecticut

How to Get There: From the east: Take I-84 West into Hartford. Merge onto Route 2 West using Exit 54 toward downtown Hartford. Route 2 turns into Founders Bridge, then into State Street. Turn left onto Columbus Boulevard and you'll see the center on the left.

GPS Coordinates: 41.7647° N, -72.6694° W

Did You Know? There are other live shows at the center, including the Wildlife Encounter Animal Stage Show and Bubblemania.

Connecticut State Capitol

Prior to the American Revolution, Hartford and New Haven alternated as Connecticut's capitol, but after the Civil War, Harford won out and a new capitol building was established. The building, which opened in 1871, is Eastlake style with elements of the French and Gothic revivals. Visitors can enjoy the main floor galleries that feature historical artifacts from both the Revolutionary War and the Civil War.

Best Time to Visit: Since the capitol is open Monday through Friday 8:00 a.m. and 5:00 p.m., year round.

Pass/Permit/Fees: There is no fee to visit or tour.

Closest City or Town: Hartford, Connecticut

How to Get There: From I-84 East: Take Exit 48 for Capitol Avenue and follow the signs to Asylum Street. Turn right onto Asylum Street and continue bearing right until you reach Pulaski Circle. Take a right onto Elm Street. Follow Elm Street to the traffic light and cross Trinity Street onto the state capitol grounds.

GPS Coordinates: 41.7642° N, -72.6825° W

Did You Know? The gold dome is covered in gold leaves and has an estimated value of $200 million. Originally, there was a large statue on top of the dome called "The Genius of Connecticut," but it was removed in 1938 following damage from the great hurricane in the same year. The statue, which was cast in bronze and made in Rome, was melted down during World War II to make ammunition and other metal parts for machines.

The Mark Twain House & Museum

Mark Twain, the pen name of Samuel Clemens, one of America's most beloved authors, witnessed the evolution of a young country from a war-torn nation to an international power. He documented his views related to westward expansion, the end of slavery, industrialization, war, and more in his novels. The most famous of his works include *The Adventures of Tom Sawyer*, *Huckleberry Finn*, and *A Connecticut Yankee in King Arthur's Court*. Twain and his wife, Olivia, moved into their Hartford house in 1874 and lived there until 1891, when financial issues forced them to move to Europe. Twain's family sold the home in 1903 after Olivia refused to return following the death of their daughter, Susy, from spinal meningitis in 1896.

Best Time to Visit: The museum is only open Friday through Monday from 10:00 a.m. to 4:30 p.m.

Pass/Permit/Fees: Adult admission is $21, and children between the ages of 6 and 16 are $13. Seniors over the age of 64 are $19, and children under 6 are free.

Closest City or Town: Hartford, Connecticut

How to Get There: From the north: Take I-91 South to I-84 West in Hartford. Take Exit 46 for Sisson Avenue, then turn right. After four blocks, turn right onto Farmington Avenue. You'll see the sign for the free parking lot on the right.

GPS Coordinates: 41.7670° N, -72.7014° W

Did You Know? The interior of the house was designed by Associated Artists and Louis C. Tiffany &. Co.

Old State House

Connecticut's Old State House is the location of the state's first legislative session, which was held on May 11, 1796. It has long been the center of government for Connecticut. It's where debates over various issues have occurred, including meeting in secret in 1815 to oppose the country's involvement in the War of 1812. The construction of the new state house was ordered in 1792 to replace the original building that was then located on the same property. At one time, the Old State House was the capitol building, but in 1878, the capitol moved into its own building. The state house became Hartford City Hall. Currently, it is a public museum that teaches visitors about Connecticut history.

Best Time to Visit: The Old State House is closed on Sunday and Monday, and open from Tuesday through Saturday between the hours of 12:00 p.m. and 5:00 p.m. (8:00 p.m. on Thursday).

Pass/Permit/Fees: Adult admission is $8, while children between the ages of 6 and 17 are $4. Children ages 5 and under are free.

Closest City or Town: Hartford, Connecticut

How to Get There: From New Haven: Take I-91 North for 36.7 miles to Whitehead Highway in Hartford. Take Exit 29A onto Whitehead Highway and drive 0.8 miles to Central Row, where the Old State House is located.

GPS Coordinates: 41.7660° N, -72.6727° W

Did You Know? The Old Statehouse reflects three distinct architectural periods: the Federal, Victorian, and Colonial Revival.

The Bushnell Performing Arts Center

Five generations of art and theater lovers have been coming to the Bushnell Performing Arts Center since its 1930 opening. Designed by Corbett, Harrison, and MacMurray two years before they designed Radio City Music Hall, the Bushnell Performing Arts Center was the brainchild of Dotha Bushnell Hillyer. Hillyer wanted to open a state-of-the-art performing arts center in memory of her father, Horace Bushnell, "as a gift to the people of Connecticut." While opening in the middle of the Great Depression was risky, it was viewed as a "beacon of hope," and has continued to thrive since then.

Best Time to Visit: The theater season runs from October to March each year, so if you want to see a show, visit during these months. However, the center is open for tours daily except for Sunday.

Pass/Permit/Fees: There is no fee to visit the Bushnell Performing Arts Center unless you decide to see a show.

Closest City or Town: Hartford, Connecticut

How to Get There: From the north or south: Take I-91 South or North to Exit 29A for the Capitol Area. Take a slight right onto Elm Street, then turn left onto West Street (the first left). Turn right onto Capitol Avenue and drive for one block, where the theater is located.

GPS Coordinates: 41.7626° N, -72.6809° W

Did You Know? Notable artists who have performed at the Bushnell Performing Arts Center include Katharine Hepburn, Mikhail Baryshnikov, Marian Anderson, and Luciano Pavarotti, among others.

Harriet Beecher Stowe Center

The interactive tour at Harriet Beecher Stowe Center, which is contained within Harriet Beecher Stowe's house, allows visitors to learn about Beecher Stowe's writings, life, travels, and family.

However, you'll also learn about 19th-century social issues that still resonate today, including slavery, the role of women, equal pay, and more. The museum features Beecher Stowe's personal items and oil paintings that she created herself. What's more is that you'll hear all about the events that led up to her writing her most famous novel, *Uncle Tom's Cabin*.

Best Time to Visit: The museum is only open Thursday from 12:30 p.m. to 8:00 p.m., Friday from 11:00 a.m. to 7:00 p.m., and Saturday from 8:30 a.m. to 5:30 p.m. It is closed the rest of the week, and Saturday is the busiest day for tours.

Pass/Permit/Fees: Admission is $20 for adults ages 18 to 64, $15 for seniors ages 65+, and $10 for children ages 6 to 16. Children under the age of 6 are free.

Closest City or Town: Hartford, Connecticut

How to Get There: From the north: Take I-95 South to I-84, then take I-84 West to Exit 46 for Sisson Avenue. Turn right onto Sisson Avenue, then right on Farmington Avenue. From there, turn right again on Forest Street, where the center is located.

GPS Coordinates: 41.7668° N, -72.7004° W

Did You Know? Beecher Stowe was an avid gardener and created numerous flower and vegetable gardens around her house. The gardens are meant to memorialize her efforts.

Mortensen Riverfront Plaza

An urban park located on the river in Hartford, Mortensen Riverfront Plaza includes a stage and seating for 2,500 spectators, public boat cruises, fishing access, sculptures, paved and lighted walkways, and more. It is the centerpiece of the nonprofit group Riverfront Recapture's efforts to make the Connecticut River more accessible to Hartford's citizens through safe and clean parks. In addition to Mortensen Riverfront Plaza, the group maintains Charter Oak Landing, Great River Park, and Riverside Park. All are open from sunrise to sunset.

Best Time to Visit: The summer is the best time to visit Mortensen Riverfront Plaza, particularly if you intend to participate in water activities.

Pass/Permit/Fees: There is no fee to visit Mortensen Riverfront Plaza.

Closest City or Town: Hartford, Connecticut

How to Get There: From the north or south: Take I-91 to Exit 29-A onto Whitehead Highway. Then, take the Columbus Boulevard exit. Turn right onto Columbus Boulevard. You will see the plaza on your right at the second traffic light.

GPS Coordinates: 41.7650° N, -72.6691° W

Did You Know? The Community Rowing Program operates in Mortenson Riverfront Plaza. It allows children and adults to compete on nationally recognized rowing teams or simply participate on a recreational level.

Museum of Connecticut History

Exhibits that feature Connecticut's role in shaping the United States and the state's own growth and development are the staples of the Museum of Connecticut History. In Memorial Hall, you'll find portraits of all 72 Connecticut governors, while in other rooms, you'll learn about the Freedom Trail, the Mitchelson Coin Collection, the legend of the Charter Oak, Colt Firearms, and much more.

Best Time to Visit: The museum is open year round on Monday through Friday from 9:00 a.m. to 4:00 p.m. and from 9:00 a.m. to 2:00 p.m. on Saturday. The best time to visit is during the week when local schools are in session, since many field trips are held at this museum.

Pass/Permit/Fees: There is no fee to visit the Museum of Connecticut History.

Closest City or Town: Hartford, Connecticut

How to Get There: From the north or south: Take I-91 to Exit 29A. At the traffic circle, take Elm Street. At the first traffic light, turn left onto Trinity Street. At the first light, you'll see the museum directly across from the state capitol building.

GPS Coordinates: 41.7626° N, -72.6830° W

Did You Know? The museum's sampler exhibit gives you a glimpse of the various artifacts, which includes the state's original manuscripts of the Declaration of Independence, an early 20th-century voting booth, weapons, and other items.

Bushnell Park

Bushnell Park is an arboretum of trees, both rare and native. Reverend Horace Bushnell and park designer Jacob Weidenmann created a natural space that includes more than 150 varieties of trees. Many of the original trees planted by these two men died over the years, both from age and neglect, but in the 1980s and 1990s, the Bushnell Park Foundation spearheaded a renovation effort that called for, in part, the planting of 400 additional trees. Other structures and objects of note in the park include the Corning Fountain, a 1914 restored carousel, the Horace Wells Statue, the Israel Putnam Statue, the Spanish-American War Memorial, and the Pump House.

Best Time to Visit: The fall is the best time to visit Bushnell Park because of the splendor of the hundreds of trees that will be changing color at that time.

Pass/Permit/Fees: There is no fee to visit Bushnell Park.

Closest City or Town: Hartford, Connecticut

How to Get There: From New Haven: Take I-91 North for 36.7 miles to Whitehead Highway in Hartford. Take Exit 29A onto Whitehead Highway and travel for 0.8 miles to Jewell Street, where the park is located.

GPS Coordinates: 41.7651° N, -72.6792° W

Did You Know? When Bushnell first approached the public about developing a new park in Hartford, the public was hesitant because he wanted to place it among leather tanneries, soapworks, pigsties, and a garbage dump. However, the park was eventually approved, making it the first municipal park in the nation.

Nipmuck State Forest

More than 9,000 acres are available for recreation in Nipmuck State Forest and the adjoining Bigelow Hollow State Park. Nipmuck State Forest is the second-oldest forest in the state, having been acquired in 1905. In this massive forest and park, you'll find a multitude of activities available, including boating, fishing, hunting, scuba diving, and picnicking. In the winter, you can cross-country ski, take a snowmobile ride, or go ice fishing. Some of the fish you may catch include trout, smallmouth bass, largemouth bass, and pickerel. There are more than 30 miles of hiking trails in the forest and park, and camping is allowed in the back country portion of the forest.

Best Time to Visit: Hunters should visit in November and December for deer season. Fall is the best time to see the foliage on the trees as they change colors.

Pass/Permit/Fees: There is no fee for residents to visit Nipmuck State Forest, but non-residents are $15 per vehicle on weekends and holidays, and $10 per vehicle on weekdays. After 4:00 p.m., the fee is reduced to $6.

Closest City or Town: Stafford Springs, Connecticut

How to Get There: Take I-84 to Exit 73, then take Route 190 North to Route 171 East, where you'll see the park's entrance.

GPS Coordinates: 42.01543° N, -72.17097° W

Did You Know? The forest gets its name from the Nipmuck Indians who lived in the area before the colonists arrived.

Bigelow Hollow State Park

As part of Nipmuck State Park, Bigelow Hollow State Park encompasses over 9,000 acres packed with recreational opportunities like hiking, fishing, boating, picnicking, cross-country skiing, scuba diving, hunting, and snowmobiling. None of the hiking trails in the park are loop trails, so if you're looking for a loop, you'll have to hike 6 miles around the Breakneck area. There are three remote backpack campsites near Briggs Pond, but they are not accessible by motor vehicle. Be sure to bring all the gear you'll need into the site on foot.

Best Time to Visit: Fall is the best time to visit Bigelow Hollow State Park for the scenery, but there are activities for visitors all year long.

Pass/Permit/Fees: There is no fee for residents to visit Bigelow Hollow State Park, but non-residents are $15 per vehicle on weekends and holidays, and $10 per vehicle on weekdays. After 4:00 p.m., the fee is reduced to $6.

Closest City or Town: Stafford Springs, Connecticut

How to Get There: Take I-84 to Exit 73, then take Route 190 North to Route 171 E, where you'll see the park's entrance.

GPS Coordinates: 41.9918° N, -72.1305° W

Did You Know? Legend says that the name Bigelow Hollow came from the name "Big Low," which referred to the hollow that created the 18-acre pond in the park. The current 300-acre lake was initially only 150 acres in size, but a battle over the lake in the 1880s ended with the parties eventually increasing the size as a compromise.

Metacomet

This 62.2-mile trail tracks the traprock ridge from Meriden to the border of Massachusetts. Expect to pass Castle Craig in Hubbard Park, the Heublein Tower in Talcott Mountain State Park, Hill-Stead Museum in Farmington, Will Warren's Den, Ragged Mountain, Suffield Mountain, and Tariffville Gorge along the route. The Metacomet Trail intersects numerous other trail systems, many of which are discussed here separately. While challenging in places, much of the trail is wide and flat, making it appropriate for hikers of most abilities.

Best Time to Visit: Blooming wildflowers in the spring and changing foliage in the fall make these two seasons the best times to hike the Metacomet Trail.

Pass/Permit/Fees: There is no fee to hike the Metacomet.

Closest City or Town: Simsbury, Connecticut

How to Get There: From Hartford: Take Main Street north toward State House Square to Chapel Street North. Turn left onto Chapel Street North. Take a slight right onto Walnut Street, then continue onto Homestead Avenue. After 1.1 miles, turn left onto Albany Avenue. Go 0.6 miles, then turn right onto Connecticut Highway 189 North/Bloomfield Avenue. Take a slight left onto Connecticut Highway 185 West/Simsbury Road. The trailhead will be on the left.

GPS Coordinates: 41.8379° N, -72.7850° W

Did You Know? The Metacomet Ridge was formed approximately 200 million years ago, during the early Jurassic period. It is composed of basalt.

Talcott Mountain

When you enter into the Farmington River Valley, you won't be able to miss the Heublein Tower at the summit of Talcott Mountain. This structure was constructed as a summer home for Gilbert Heublein in 1914. A hike up the 1,000-foot mountain will not only allow you to explore this landmark, but also provide you with splendid views of the Farmington River Valley. You'll even be able to see all the way to Mount Monadnock in New Hampshire, a distance of 80 miles! Varied wildlife, including foxes, deer, and rabbits, may make an appearance during your hike.

Best Time to Visit: To see wildflowers like trout lily, wood anemone, trillium, and Dutchman's breeches, visit Talcott Mountain in May.

Pass/Permit/Fees: There is no fee to visit Talcott Mountain.

Closest City or Town: Bloomfield, Connecticut

How to Get There: From the north or south: Take I-91 to Exit 35B for Route 218 in Bloomfield. Take Route 218/Cottage Grove Road west to Route 185. Take Route 185 toward Simsbury. You'll see the entrance to Talcott Mountain State Park on the left at the top of the hill.

GPS Coordinates: 41.83918° N, -72.78790° W

Did You Know? Two future presidents stayed at Heublein Tower in the early 1950s. Then-General Dwight D. Eisenhower was asked to run for president during his visit, and later, then-president of the Screen Actors Guild, Ronald Reagan, visited as a guest of the *Hartford Times*.

Ragged Mountain

This mountain ridge is located just west of New Britain, Connecticut and is part of the Metacomet Ridge that spans the Long Island Sound and the Connecticut River Valley to the Vermont border. There are numerous popular hiking trails on Ragged Mountain, and it draws rock climbers from all over the country to scale its vertical cliff faces. The 51-mile Metacomet Trail crosses Ragged Mountain, which also takes hikers to Bradley Mountain and Short Mountain. The peak of Ragged Mountain is 500 feet above the Quinnipiac River Valley.

Best Time to Visit: Fall is the best time to hike Ragged Mountain because you'll avoid the mud and water of the spring, and you'll get to see some spectacular foliage colors as well.

Pass/Permit/Fees: There is no cost to visit Ragged Mountain.

Closest City or Town: Berlin, Connecticut

How to Get There:
From Hartford: Travel along I-84 for 12.6 miles to New Britain, then take Exit 7 onto Connecticut Highway 372 East/Corbin Avenue. Continue for 5.5 miles to Ragged Mountain Road and the trailhead.

GPS Coordinates: 41.62894° N, -72.80377° W

Did You Know? You can snowshoe on Ragged Mountain in the winter, but know that the Blue and Red Loop is rockier than the orange trail. However, the Blue and Red Loop features more rock formations, vernal pools, a waterfall, and amazing cliff face views.

Enders State Forest

Waterfalls, easy hikes, swimming, and cliff jumping are all favorite activities to engage in at Enders State Park. There are several trails leading to various waterfalls from the parking lot, and all meet up at a maintained gravel path alongside Enders Brook. A number of the falls can be seen from the road, or you can make your way to a viewing platform to see the second waterfall and cliffs. There are 2,100 acres in the forest. The original 1,500 acres were gifted to the state in memory of John Ostrom Enders and Harriet Whitmore in 1970. Follow the trail marked with purple blazes to reach the viewing areas.

Best Time to Visit: While the waterfalls flow best in the spring, a great time to visit the forest for spectacular photos is in the fall when the leaves have begun to change color.

Pass/Permit/Fees: There is no fee to visit Enders State Forest.

Closest City or Town: Granby, Connecticut

How to Get There: From Granby: Take Route 219 (Barkhamsted Road) south for 1.3 miles. You will see the entrance to the forest to the left.

GPS Coordinates: 41.95963° N, -72.88356° W

Did You Know? When the forest land was donated to the state of Connecticut, there was a stipulation that there be no hunting on the land. As a result, visitors may see a variety of wildlife in the area, since their forest habitat is preserved for their well-being.

Enders Falls

This waterfall is located within the boundaries of Enders State Forest, which is a massive 2,103 acres in size. Enders Falls is just one of the many attractions in the forest. However, Enders Falls is popular for both visitors and locals because of the relatively easy hike to the top, swimming in the basin, and cliff jumping from the surrounding heights. The hike to the falls is just 0.5 miles and follows a well-marked path of stone steps and wood rail fencing. There is a small viewing platform along the way, where you'll get a spectacular image of the second waterfall before you reach the top of the main waterfall.

Best Time to Visit: The falls flow best in the spring, when the snowmelt makes the waters high and free flowing. However, the cool water presents a nice way to beat the heat in the summers as well.

Pass/Permit/Fees: There is no fee to visit Enders State Forest.

Closest City or Town: Granby, Connecticut

How to Get There: From Granby: Take Route 219 (Barkhamsted Road) south for 1.3 miles. You will see the entrance to the forest to the left.

GPS Coordinates: 41.9597° N, -72.8837° W

Did You Know? Enders Falls is comprised of five distinct waterfalls, including the first with a 6-foot cascade, the second with a 30-foot horsetail and plunge cascade, the third with an 18-foot horsetail and plunge cascade, the fourth with a 12-foot plunge cascade, and the fifth with a two-segment plunge cascade.

Saville Dam

Located on the Farmington River, Saville Dam is an earth and masonry embankment dam that creates the Barkhamsted Reservoir. Construction began in 1936, and it was originally called the Bill's Brook Dam for the brook that passed near the area at the time. The dam was completed in 1940 and was renamed the Saville Dam after Caleb Mills Saville, the chief engineer on the project. The dam holds back 36.8 billion gallons of water and provides the primary water source for Hartford, Connecticut.

Best Time to Visit: The many trees on the dam make this an awesome place to visit when the leaves are changing colors in the fall.

Pass/Permit/Fees: There is no fee to visit the Saville Dam, and the road that goes over the dam is a public road that is open 24 hours a day.

Closest City or Town: Barkhamsted, Connecticut

How to Get There: From Hartford: Take Homestead Avenue 2.2 miles to US-44 West/Albany Avenue. Follow US-44 West for 16.5 miles to Wickett Street in New Hartford. Take Connecticut Highway 219 North to Lake McDonough in Barkhamsted, where you'll see the dam.

GPS Coordinates: 41.90916° N, -72.95888° W

Did You Know? Even though the dam was completed in 1940, it took until 1948 for the Barkhamsted Reservoir to fill to capacity. At this time, the reservoir flooded a number of farms in Barkhamsted. You can see the remains of Barkhamsted Center just to the west of the reservoir.

Farmington River

Located in the northwest corner of the state, the Farmington River is a part of the National Wild and Scenic River System that was established in 1968 to protect rivers from damming, hydroelectric facilities, and other projects. Tubers will find a variety of rapids ranging from class I to class III, with the more challenging spots located at Satan's Kingdom Recreation Area. Fishing is also a popular activity on the river, as bass, pike, carp, and trout are abundant and large.

Best Time to Visit: Since the water in the Farmington River stays cool even during the hottest days of the year, summer is the best time to visit for tubing and boating. Spring is the best time to visit for fly fishing.

Pass/Permit/Fees: The Farmington River is free to visit, but if you rent a tube to ride the rapids, you'll pay $20 per person on weekends and holidays, and $18 per person on weekdays.

Closest City or Town: Farmington, Connecticut

How to Get There: From Hartford: Take Main Street north toward State House Square and continue onto US-44 West/Albany Ave. Travel for 8.9 miles to US-202 East. Take US-202 East for 2.1 miles to Talcott Acres Road. Travel for 0.3 miles to the river.

GPS Coordinates: 41.85964° N, -72.95910° W (These coordinates will take you to Farmington River Tubing off of Main Street.)

Did You Know? The Farmington River Valley is currently the only place in the state with nesting bald eagles.

National Iwo Jima Memorial

The Iwo Jima Survivors Association erected the National Iwo Jima Memorial in New Britain and Newington, Connecticut in 1995 to commemorate the 50th anniversary of the event. The memorial was commissioned to remember the 6,821 US servicemen who died during the Battle of Iwo Jima in Japan in 1945. The names of the 100 men from Connecticut who lost their lives in that battle are inscribed on the base of the memorial. This memorial, which is 40 feet high and includes a 48-star flag for historical accuracy, is the only one in existence that was built by Iwo Jima Survivors.

Best Time to Visit: The National Iwo Jima Memorial is open year round, but summer is the busiest time of year for visits. If you prefer a less crowded visit, choose spring or fall instead.

Pass/Permit/Fees: There is no fee to visit the National Iwo Jima Memorial.

Closest City or Town: New Britain, Connecticut

How to Get There: From Hartford: Take I-84 for 8.7 miles to Newington. Take Exit 29 and turn left on Ella Grasso Road. The memorial will be on the right.

GPS Coordinates: 41.6982° N, -72.7586° W

Did You Know? The rocks that are situated beneath the memorial at the feet of the soldiers raising the flag are from the original site on Mt. Suribachi, and volcanic sand from Iwo Jima is mixed into the concrete base, which means this is the only memorial of its kind.

Tunxis Trail

This 38.5-mile trail is the main part of a larger trail system comprised of 19 trails and 83 miles. The southern end of the Tunxis Trail is located in Southington, and it runs north to the Massachusetts border. The diverse terrain and landscapes that hikers encounter while on this trail make it a popular hike. The incredible views from Norton Outlook and Julian's Rock are worth the effort to hike the entire 38.5 miles. Be sure to look for the Mile of Ledges, the Tory Den, and other features along the way. If you don't have time to hike the full trail, there are plenty of well-marked opportunities to loop back to where you started.

Best Time to Visit: For wildflower viewing, spring is the best time to visit the Tunxis Trail.

Pass/Permit/Fees: There is no fee to hike the Tunxis Trail.

Closest City or Town: Bristol, Connecticut

How to Get There: From Hartford: Merge onto I-84 and follow for 7.5 miles. Take Exit 38 for US-6 West toward Bristol. Keep left to continue on US-6 West, then follow signs for US-6 East. Turn right onto Mix Street. Continue onto Maple Avenue, which turns into Peacedale Street, then continue onto James P Casey Road. Turn right onto Battle Street. Continue straight onto Hill Street for 0.8 miles and then W. Chippens Hill Road for 0.7 miles. Turn left onto Greer Road. The trail head will be on the left in 0.2 miles.

GPS Coordinates: 41.72486° N, -72.99110° W

Did You Know? The Tunxis Trail is broken up over the full 83 miles. In Wolcott, Harwinton, New Hartford, and Plymouth, you'll find 17 other trails.

Litchfield Hills

Litchfield Hills is a collection of villages, waterfalls, covered bridges, hiking trails, and other iconic New England features located in the northwest corner of Connecticut. From this area, you can hike the Appalachian Trail, visit one of the many postcard-picture towns, pick fruit from a farm, kayak down a river, or simply view the incredible fall foliage. This is a place you go for quiet relaxation, where the height of adventure is connecting with nature. You won't run out of things to do, especially if you're into exploring vast open areas and tiny bucolic towns.

Best Time to Visit: Litchfield Hills is best visited in the fall when all the trees are magnificently changing colors.

Pass/Permit/Fees: There is no fee to visit Litchfield Hills.

Closest City or Town: Torrington, Connecticut

How to Get There: Take I-84 for 32.9 miles to Milton Road in Litchfield. Turn right onto Milton Road and travel 2.8 miles to Maple Street. Turn right onto Maple Street and drive to Kubish Road.

GPS Coordinates: 41.79423° N, -73.21166° W (These coordinates will take you to the historical town's central green.)

Did You Know? You're likely to find some amazing craft beers in Litchfield Hills, as it has become a favorite destination among beer connoisseurs. Local breweries provide beer tastings, live music, and meals from famous food trucks. You might even get roped into playing disc golf or going on a mountain bike ride while you're there!

Burr Pond State Park

Burr Pond State Park is a recreational area that spans 438 acres, of which 85 acres is the man-made Burr Pond. Swimming, fishing, and boating are all popular activities in the park. Anglers can expect to catch largemouth bass, black crappie, bluegill, chain pickerel, yellow perch, and brown bullhead. There is also a 2.25-mile hiking loop around the pond and another 2-mile trail that connects Burr Pond State Park with Sunnybrook State Park.

Best Time to Visit: The summer and fall are the best times to visit Burr Pond State Park, especially if you want to participate in water sports.

Pass/Permit/Fees: There is no fee for residents to visit Burr Pond State Park, but non-residents are $15 per vehicle on weekends and holidays. All visitors are free on weekdays.

Closest City or Town: Torrington, Connecticut

How to Get There: From Route 8 North: Take Exit 46 and turn left onto Pinewoods Road. Take Pinewoods Road to the first light, then turn left onto Winsted Road. Follow this road for about 1 mile and turn right at the light onto Burr Mountain Road. After another mile, you'll see the park's entrance.

GPS Coordinates: 41.8698° N, -73.0937° W

Did You Know? The first condensed milk factory in the world was built on Burr Pond land in 1857 by Gail Borden, the person who discovered how to preserve milk. This product became vital to the Union Army during the Civil War. The mill was destroyed by a fire in 1877.

Campbell Falls State Park

A 50-foot waterfall is the centerpiece of Campbell Falls State Park, but there is also a moderate hiking trail available, along with stream fishing for trout. The waterfall is one of the most forceful in the state, making a thunderous sound in the spring when the water is at its highest and fastest. The hike to the falls is short and only somewhat challenging, particularly in the spring when the terrain might be wet. A wooden bridge that crosses the river makes an excellent backdrop for photos and selfies.

Best Time to Visit: Spring is the best time to visit Campbell Falls State Park if you want to experience the full effect of the falls rushing through the gorge.

Pass/Permit/Fees: There is no fee to visit Campbell Falls State Park.

Closest City or Town: Torrington, Connecticut

How to Get There: From Norfolk: Take Route 272 North to Old Spaulding Road. The park's entrance is on the right.

GPS Coordinates: 42.04293° N, -73.22436° W (These coordinates take you to the Campbells Falls Trail.)

Did You Know? In the middle of the hiking trail, you'll pass into Massachusetts. There is a stone pillar marking the border between the two states. You'll get the best view of the falls on the Massachusetts side of the park, but it can be seen from several points on the trail. The reason these falls are so loud is because they pass through a tight gorge that magnifies the noise of the rushing water.

Steep Rock Preserve

For one of the best hiking experiences in Connecticut, visit the 998-acre Steep Rock Preserve, where its miles of hiking trails track the Shepaug River and give hikers access to the hillsides above. You'll find the remnants of carriage roads at the Preserve's north end. One of them will take you to the Holiday House, a former country retreat that offered a respite from the city to working-class women living in New York City at the turn of the 20th century. A railroad tunnel cut through the rock ledge can also be viewed from the trail.

Best Time to Visit: The best time to visit Steep Rock Preserve and hike the trail is between March and October, although some people may find the summer heat to be too intense for the 4.2-mile trail.

Pass/Permit/Fees: There is no fee to hike, but the overnight camping fee is $35 per night.

Closest City or Town: Washington Depot, Connecticut

How to Get There: From Hartford: Take I-84 for 31.6 miles to Connecticut Highway 64 West/Chase Parkway. Take Exit 17 onto Connecticut 64 West. Continue for 19.9 miles to the preserve's entrance.

GPS Coordinates: 41.62073° N, -73.32322° W

Did You Know? Pennsylvanian coal miners built the railroad tunnel on the preserve, which was completed in 1872 as a section of the Shepaug Valley Railroad. They used dynamite, hand picks, and nitroglycerin to blast through the rocky hillside. It only took only nine months to complete. The railroad ended service in 1948.

Yellow Circle Blazes Loop

This popular 3.7-mile hiking loop is a moderately challenging trail located near Washington Depot, Connecticut. The path follows the Shepaug River part of the way. While the first mile of the trail is appropriate for horseback riders, the final 2.7 miles are more strenuous, and horses are prohibited. Also known as Steep Rock Loop for its location in Steep Rock Preservation, hikers should follow the yellow-circle blazes to stay on the trail. The terrain and scenery along the way are diverse, which makes this trail a favorite among locals. Be sure to bring your camera to take awe-inspiring photos of the suspension bridges and waterways along the route.

Best Time to Visit: In the fall, you'll get gorgeous views of the changing foliage, but be sure to visit in the mornings because it gets crowded in the afternoons.

Pass/Permit/Fees: There is no fee to hike Yellow Circle Blazes Loop.

Closest City or Town: Washington Depot, Connecticut

How to Get There: From the north or south: Take US-202 to Connecticut Highway 47 into Washington Depot. Take a left onto Main Street No. 1. Follow Main Street No. 1 to the end of the road, then turn right onto River Road. You'll see the trailhead at the three-way intersection of River Road, Tunnel Road, and Church Hill Road.

GPS Coordinates: 41.6208° N, 73.3232° W

Did You Know? Before or after you hike the trail, explore the Railroad Tunnel, which is a 235-foot carved arch that was constructed by the Shepaug Valley Railroad.

Lake Waramaug

For photographers, a more picturesque lake won't be found in the state, particularly in the fall when the changing colors are reflected in the calm waters of Lake Waramaug. Other activities in this state park include camping, boating, picnicking, fishing, swimming, canoeing, and kayaking. There are 77 campsites in the park, both in open areas and more secluded wooded settings. Camping is available between Memorial Day weekend and September 30.

Best Time to Visit: Campers should visit between Memorial Day weekend and September 30, but photographers will get the best shots in the fall when the leaves are changing.

Pass/Permit/Fees: There is no fee for residents to visit Lake Waramaug at any time, but non-residents will be charged $15 per vehicle on weekends and holidays. Weekdays are free for all visitors.

Closest City or Town: New Preston, Connecticut

How to Get There: From New Milford: Take Route 202 to New Preston and turn left onto Route 45. Take Route 45 to North Shore Road and turn left. Follow the signs to the park's entrance.

GPS Coordinates: 41.70926° N, -73.38620° W

Did You Know? The name *Waramaug* comes from a Wyantenock Indian tribe chief who hunted near the Housatonic River in the town of New Milford. Chief Waramaug and his tribe spent winters by modern-day Lake Lillinonah and summers at Lake Waramaug.

Bantam Lake

Bantam Lake, the largest natural lake in the state, is home to Morris Town Beach and Sandy Beach in Litchfield. Sandy Beach is known for its canoe launch and picnic facilities, while Morris Town Beach is smaller in size and excellent for hanging out by the water. The Bantam Lake Ski Club, the oldest continuously operating club for water skiers in the U.S., calls the lake home, as does the Litchfield Hills Rowing Club. High school students and adults can take rowing classes and programs in the summer and fall from the Litchfield Hills Rowing Club.

Best Time to Visit: While the lake is open year round, the best time to visit for water sports is the summer and fall.

Pass/Permit/Fees: There is no fee to visit Bantam Lake.

Closest City or Town: Litchfield, Connecticut

How to Get There: From Hartford: Take I-84 for 12.7 miles to Plainville, then take Exit 33 onto Connecticut Highway 72 West. Follow Connecticut 72 for 9 miles to Main Street in Plymouth. Follow Main Street for 5.5 miles to Connecticut Highway 109 West in Thomaston. Travel for 10 miles to Heron Pointe Road and the lake.

GPS Coordinates: Morris Town Beach: 41.68990° N, -73.22384° W
Sandy Beach: 41.70634° N, -73.20991° W
Litchfield Town Beach: 41.71809° N, -73.21712° W

Did You Know? The northern end of Bantam Lake is protected by White Memorial Foundation, as it is home to numerous bird species. This includes Marsh Point Peninsula.

Mattatuck Trail

This 42-mile trail consists of a woodland footpath that winds beside streams and passes by ponds, a cave, and waterfalls. It begins at Wolcott in the south, then crosses the White Memorial Conservation Center, Mattatuck State Forest, Black Rock State Park, Shepaug Reservoir land, and Mohawk State Forest before climbing Mohawk Mountain and ending at Mohawk Trail. From various points along the trail, you'll get amazing views of reservoirs, marshes, and woodlands, making it a photographer's dream.

Best Time to Visit: To see wildflowers in bloom, the best time to visit is during the spring, but to see the colorful foliage, the best time to visit is in the fall. Take care to wear bright colors during hunting season, since hunting is allowed in the forests you'll pass through.

Pass/Permit/Fees: There is no fee to hike the Mattatuck Trail.

Closest City or Town: Litchfield, Connecticut

How to Get There: From Hartford: Take I-84 for 11.9 miles to Farmington. Take New Britain Avenue for 22.5 miles to East Street in Litchfield. Continue onto US-202 West/West Street to Constitution Way. After 1.9 miles, you'll see the trailhead.

GPS Coordinates: 41.71973° N, -73.20255° W

Did You Know? The best way to experience this incredible hike is to park one vehicle at the end and one at the beginning. That way, you won't have to hike back to your car if you get tired during the long journey.

Riga Falls

Located in Mt. Riga State Park, Riga Falls is one of the lesser-known waterfalls in the state. The shallow swimming pool at the bottom of the falls is perfect for floating in the cool waters during the summer. Since it's not a prominent tourist attraction, you're likely to be the only one there, and you can enjoy the sounds of nature as you take in the cascading falls and the surrounding woods. The falls are located near the dirt path, but you will need to leave the road to find them. As this is a hidden gem, be prepared to use your ears to help you navigate and explore!

Best Time to Visit: The falls run fast and full during the spring with the annual snow melt, but the watering hole is ideal as a cool-off spot in the summer as well.

Pass/Permit/Fees: There is no fee to visit this park, or Riga Falls within it.

Closest City or Town: Salisbury, Connecticut

How to Get There: From Salisbury: Take Connecticut Highway 41 North to US-44 West. Turn left on US-44 West. Drive 0.2 miles to Factory-Washinee and turn right. Stay on Factory Street until you see Mt. Riga Road. Take a slight right onto Mt. Riga Road, then travel 2.3 miles to the park's entrance.

GPS Coordinates: 42.03369° N, -73.42985° W

Did You Know? The entire Mt. Riga State Park is 276 acres and is one of the few undeveloped parks in the state. There are paths throughout the park, but they are unpaved, and in most cases, unmarked. The hike to the top of the falls can be slippery, especially if it has just rained.

Bear Mountain Trail

This is an extremely popular hiking trail that takes hikers to the summit of Bear Mountain, which is the highest peak in Connecticut (2,316 feet). It is rated as challenging, so it's not a trail for beginners or even some intermediate hikers. It is 5.4 miles out and back, so plan to spend a couple of hours exploring the area. The trail offers outstanding views, especially in the fall, and on a clear day, you may be able to see the mountains in southern New Hampshire. At the summit, there are the remains of a stone tower that was built in 1885 to mark the highest point in the state.

Best Time to Visit: The best months to visit Bear Mountain Trail is between March and November, with gorgeous wildflowers in the spring and awe-inspiring foliage in the fall.

Pass/Permit/Fees: There is no fee to hike Bear Mountain Trail.

Closest City or Town: Salisbury, Connecticut

How to Get There: From Hartford: Take US-44 West for 47.9 miles to Egremont Road in Sheffield. Take Egremont Road for 3.6 miles to MA-23 West/MA-41 South in Egremont. Take Mount Washington Road for 11.8 miles to Mount Washington Road in Salisbury. The trailhead is clearly marked.

GPS Coordinates: 42.04723° N, -73.45553° W

Did You Know? Even though Bear Mountain has the highest peak in Connecticut, the highest point in Connecticut is actually on Mount Frissell, which is just to the northwest of Bear Mountain.

Mount Frissell

Mount Frissell straddles the border of Connecticut and Massachusetts. While the peak is located in Massachusetts, the southern slope provides Connecticut's highest point of elevation at 2,379 feet. The easiest way to reach this high point is to climb nearby Bear Mountain and cross over to Mount Frissell using a short trail that connects the two mountains. The rivers on the Connecticut side of the mountain eventually reach the Housatonic River and the Long Island Sound. The Mount Frissell Trail, which runs across the mountain, connects with the South Taconic Trail in the west and the Appalachian Trail in the east.

Best Time to Visit: If your goal is to see the famed New England foliage, fall is the best time to visit Mount Frissell.

Pass/Permit/Fees: There is no fee to visit Mount Frissell.

Closest City or Town: Salisbury, Connecticut

How to Get There: From Hartford: Take US-44 West for 47.9 miles to Sheffield. Take Egremont Road to MA-23 West/MA-41 South in Egremont. Travel for 4.1 miles to Mount Washington Road to Salisbury and the trailhead.

GPS Coordinates: 42.0512° N, -73.4821° W

Did You Know? The high point of Mount Frissell is one of just three state high points that are not the summit of a mountain.

Cathedral Pines

Cathedral Pines contains the remnants of what used to be the largest old-growth white pine and hemlock tree stand in New England, boasting 42 acres of trees. These woods were protected from logging as early as 1800 despite the fact that Connecticut relied on timber for its economy. It became a favorite tourist attraction in the late 19th century and could be found on state postcards as early as 1900. In 1982, the location was declared a National Natural Landmark that would continue to protect the trees and allow them to decay naturally.

Best Time to Visit: To avoid the cold weather, the best time to visit Cathedral Pines is between April and October.

Pass/Permit/Fees: There is no fee to visit Cathedral Pines.

Closest City or Town: West Cornwall, Connecticut

How to Get There: From Hartford: Take I-84 and Connecticut Highway 4 West for 40.6 miles to Great Hollow Road in Cornwall. Continue onto Great Hollow Road and drive to Essex Hill Road, where you'll see a sign for the entrance.

GPS Coordinates: 41.8365° N, -73.3272° W

Did You Know? In July 1989, a large tornado struck Cathedral Pines, destroying the old-growth forest and numerous buildings in Cornwall Village and on Mohawk Mountain. Approximately 75% of the trees in Cathedral Pines were knocked down in a period of 20 minutes. The Nature Conservancy elected to allow the forest to regenerate naturally, and the trees were not harvested for timber.

Kent Falls State Park

Located in the northeastern part of the state, Kent Falls State Park features several waterfalls on the Falls Brook stream. This stream begins in Warren and flows west to a 70-foot waterfall appropriately called "the big fall." From there, the stream continues to flow west to the valley, creating several smaller falls along the way. There is a quarter-mile trail to the top of the falls, and while it's not a challenging path, it is steep. You'll enjoy several scenic views as you hike the trail.

Best Time to Visit: Since the waters flow the heaviest and fastest in the spring with the snowmelt, the best time to visit Kent Falls State Park is the spring. However, you can still get dramatic views of the falls after a summer rainstorm.

Pass/Permit/Fees: There is no charge to visit Kent Falls State Park for residents. For non-residents, the charge is $15 per vehicle on the weekends and holidays, and $10 per vehicle on weekdays.

Closest City or Town: Kent, Connecticut

How to Get There: From Hartford: Take I-84 West to Exit 39. Take Route 4 West to the intersection of Route 4 and Route 118. Head west on Route 118 to Route 202. Turn left on Route 202 and travel about 7 miles to route 341. Turn right on Route 341 and travel to Route 7. Turn north on Route 7 and drive for 4.5 miles to the park's entrance.

GPS Coordinates: 41.7763° N, -73.4179° W

Did You Know? Native Americans camped and fished in this area, which they called *Scatacook*.

Macedonia Brook State Park

Visitors to Macedonia Brook State Park will be treated to incredible views of the Taconics and Catskills Mountains, especially in the fall when the foliage is changing colors. There are numerous hiking trails in the park, with the Blue Trail crossing Cobble Mountain and a number of other peaks. This 2,300-acre park offers numerous outdoor activities such as camping, picnicking, stream fishing, cross-country skiing, and exploring historic sites. There is also a sports field that is used for various games and matches throughout the year. Note that dogs are not allowed at this state park.

Best Time to Visit: The best views of the mountains occur in the fall, when the leaves are changing colors.

Pass/Permit/Fees: There is no fee to visit Macedonia Brook State Park unless you plan to camp overnight.

Closest City or Town: Kent, Connecticut

How to Get There: Take Route 341 West from the center of Kent. Turn right onto Macedonia Brook Road. At Fuller Mountain Road, keep left and look for signs that lead to the park's entrance.

GPS Coordinates: 41.76695° N, -73.49547° W

Did You Know? The Scatacook Indians once roamed the land that is now the Macedonia Brook State Park. This is one of the few areas where Indians and settlers lived in harmony after Kent was established in 1738. In fact, the Scatacook Indians helped colonists during the Revolutionary War by operating a signal system in the mountains.

Appalachian Trail

There are 50.5 miles of the 2,200-mile Appalachian Trail that pass through Connecticut, much of which take hikers through various hardwood forests. Ned K. Anderson, the CFPA chair of the Housatonic Valley between 1929 and 1932, originally blazed the Connecticut route. The southern end of the Connecticut section of the trail begins in Sherman, Connecticut and ends in Salisbury, just north of the Massachusetts border. It crosses the Housatonic River twice, and the trail is known for its rocky hills, ravines, valleys, waterfalls, and, of course, majestic views.

Best Time to Visit: If you're looking to avoid crowds, hike the trail between April and May, but if you want to see the fabled New England foliage, hike it during the fall.

Pass/Permit/Fees: There is no fee or permit required to hike the Connecticut portion of the Appalachian Trail.

Closest City or Town: Sherman, Connecticut

How to Get There: From Hartford: Take I-84 39.9 miles to US-6 E in Southbury. Take Exit 15 onto Connecticut Highway 67 W. Travel 25.1 miles to Connecticut Highway 55, where you'll see signs for the Appalachian Trail in Sherman.

GPS Coordinates: 41.6446° N, -73.5192° W

Did You Know? There is a three-quarter-mile portion of the Appalachian Trail in Connecticut that follows the Housatonic River. The first segment of the trail built to be accessible by everyone, this flat section is below a 50-foot waterfall. It used to be the location of a large ironworks.

Tory's Cave

Tory's Cave, though small, is believed to be the only real cave in the state. To protect and research the local bat colony, the cave can be closed during some times of the year, usually between November and April. However, it can be off limits to the public at other times as well. The largest room of the cave is only the size of a large truck, and the opening to the room is extremely tight, especially for large adults. It will require some fortitude and fearlessness to descend to the space inside, but it does provide a challenge for experienced spelunkers. Note that this is not a commercial cave and should not be explored alone.

Best Time to Visit: Since the cave is usually closed in the winter, the best times to visit are the spring, summer, and fall.

Pass/Permit/Fees: There is no fee to visit Tory's Cave.

Closest City or Town: New Milford, Connecticut

How to Get There: From Hartford: Take I-894 for 40 miles to Exit 15, then take Connecticut Highway 67 West to US-7 North in New Milford. Arrive at the preserve where the cave is located.

GPS Coordinates: 41.61995° N, -73.46206° W

Did You Know? The name of this cave refers to its history as a hideout for loyalists to England during the American Revolution. As they were referred to as Tories, this obscure hole in the ground became known as Tory's Cave.

The Aldrich Contemporary Art Museum

Founded in 1964 by art collector Larry Aldrich, this museum is one of the oldest contemporary art museums in the country. It is a non-collecting institution and is one of the few independent museums in the United States. It has the distinction of being the only museum in Connecticut that is entirely dedicated to showcasing contemporary art. The museum is housed in the "Old Hundred" building, which was constructed in 1783 by soldiers in the Revolutionary War. Originally, it was a grocery store, then later a hardware store and Ridgefield's first post office. In 1883, the house was remodeled and used as a home for Grace King Ingersoll.

Best Time to Visit: The museum is open Sunday through Friday from 12:00 p.m. to 5:00 (except on Tuesday, when it's closed), and from 10:00 a.m. to 5:00 p.m. on Saturday. Fall is a wonderful time to visit to see the changing leaves of the trees surrounding the property.

Pass/Permit/Fees: Adult admission is $12; seniors and students are $7; and children under the age of 13 are free.

Closest City or Town: Ridgefield, Connecticut

How to Get There: From Hartford: Take I-84 for 58.5 miles to US-7 in Danbury. Take Exit 3 onto US-7 South, then follow Connecticut Highway 35 South/Danbury Road to Main Street, where the museum is located.

GPS Coordinates: 41.2771° N, -73.4970° W

Did You Know? Don't forget to visit the 2-acre sculpture garden that surrounds the museum. It is open to the public and entirely free.

Keeler Tavern Museum and History Center

This 4-acre campus located in Ridgefield provides cultural and educational programs that allow guests to trace the area's history from the colonial area through the mid-20th century. Artifacts onsite include prints, paintings, sculptures, and more. Keeler Tavern, which was originally a house in 1713, then an inn in 1772, was a major gathering place for the citizens of Ridgefield in the 19th century.

Best Time to Visit: The Museum and History Center is open year round Thursday through Sunday from 11:00 a.m. to 4:00 p.m., and on Mondays from 5:00 p.m. to 8:00 p.m. Even when the museum isn't open, the grounds are open to the public as long as there are no private events.

Pass/Permit/Fees: Adult admission is $15, and children under the age of 18 are $5. Educators, veterans, and students are also $5, and seniors ages 65 and older are $12.

Closest City or Town: Ridgefield, Connecticut

How to Get There: From Hartford: Take I-84 for 23.8 miles to State Highway 101 in Cheshire. Take Exit 26 and travel 3.6 miles to Waterbury. Continue for 31.1 miles to Exit 3, then take US-7 South for 8.2 miles to Main Street in Ridgefield, where the museum is located.

GPS Coordinates: 41.2730° N, -73.4971° W

Did You Know? One notable visitor to the tavern was Jerome Bonaparte, youngest brother to Napoleon, who visited in 1804.

Philip Johnson Glass House

Built in 1949, the Philip Johnson Glass House is a 55-foot-long by 33-foot-wide glass pavilion that allows people inside the structure to view the surrounding landscape, which includes a pond and a wooded area. The Glass House is the iconic structure of the International Style that first appeared in the U.S. in the 1940s. There are no walls inside the house, but there are rectangular areas that Johnson referred to as "rooms."

Best Time to Visit: You'll get great views of Connecticut from the Glass House in the fall when you can see the changing color of the leaves. The grounds are open from April to December and closed on Tuesdays and Wednesdays.

Pass/Permit/Fees: A grounds pass to the Philip Johnson Glass House is $20 per person. Hour-long tours are an extra $25 on weekdays and $30 on weekends, and two-hour tours are $50 on weekdays and $60 on weekends.

Closest City or Town: New Canaan, Connecticut

How to Get There: From the north: Take I-95 South to Exit 11 and turn right on Boston Post Road/Route 1. Turn left onto Mansfield Avenue and drive five miles to the New Canaan town center. Turn left onto Elm Street, where the house is located.

GPS Coordinates: 41.1464° N, -73.4968° W

Did You Know? Philip Johnson conceived of the idea of a glass house as part of an artistic composition, the second component of which is the Brick House, also situated on this property.

Diane's Books

Located in Greenwich, Diane's Books is a local institution that has the biggest selection of family books in the United States. If you're looking for a book, whether it's the newest bestseller or an obscure children's book, Diane's Books will have it in stock. The staff members at this bookstore, including Diane herself, are experts at finding the right book for everyone who comes through the doors. They are book lovers and want their guests to fall in love with reading as well. Personalized service is their passion, so don't expect to leave without a hand-picked book just for you!

Best Time to Visit: Diane's Books is open Monday through Saturday from 9:00 a.m. to 5:00 p.m. If you want a quiet browsing session, choose a weekday over a Saturday.

Pass/Permit/Fees: There is no fee to visit Diane's Books.

Closest City or Town: Greenwich, Connecticut

How to Get There: From Hartford: Take I-91 South for 80.5 miles to Arch Street in Greenwich. Take Exit 3 onto Arch Street and follow it for 0.5 miles to Grigg Street, where the bookstore is located.

GPS Coordinates: 41.0170° N, -73.6217° W

Did You Know? Diane's Books opened in 1990 to fill a hole in the independent bookstore scene after Diane Garrett learned that none of the existing seven bookstores catered to children's books. Three decades later, it's the only independent bookstore left in town.

Fjord Fish Market

For some of the freshest seafood in New England, visit the Fjord Fish Market, which only offers responsibly sourced premium seafood for the best experience possible. Every seafood item in their case is labeled with maps and sourcing information so that customers know exactly what they are consuming when they purchase seafood from the market. You'll find everything from fresh Maine lobster, shrimp, salmon, and sushi to chicken, beef tenderloin, and burgers on the menu, all of which are sure to be your next favorite dish.

Best Time to Visit: Fjord Fish Market is open Monday through Saturday from 8:00 a.m. and 7:00 p.m. On Sunday, it's open between 9:00 a.m. and 6:00 p.m. The food is always fresh, but it's best to buy it in the early morning.

Pass/Permit/Fees: There is no fee to visit Fjord Fish Market, but if you want to try any of the items on their menu, you'll pay market price.

Closest City or Town: Greenwich, Connecticut

How to Get There:
From Hartford: Take I-91 South for 79.6 miles to US-1 South in Greenwich. Take Exit 5 onto US-1 and follow for 1.3 miles to the market.

GPS Coordinates: 41.03862° N, -73.60046° W

Did You Know? If you get your seafood to go from Fjord Fish Market, be sure to ask the fishmonger for a simple home recipe to help you get the best flavor from your food. They will happily provide you with preparation instructions to get the perfect meal.

Flinn Gallery

The Flinn Gallery, located in the Greenwich Library, offers five or six curated art exhibits per year from September through June. The gallery has been in Greenwich since 1928, when librarian Isabelle Hurlbutt established a space for local artists to display their work. The gallery had no name at that time. It was originally located on Greenwich Avenue, but moved to West Putnam Avenue in 1960, where it was named the Hurlbutt Gallery. The Gallery was then redesigned in 1999 and renamed the Flinn Gallery to honor Stephanie and Lawrence Flinn, premier donors to the project.

Best Time to Visit: The Flinn Gallery is only open between September and June, so these are the best months to visit.

Pass/Permit/Fees: There is no fee to visit the Flinn Gallery.

Closest City or Town: Greenwich, Connecticut

How to Get There: From Hartford: Take I-91 South for 77.1 miles to North Street in Greenwich. Take Exit 31 onto North Street and drive 5.1 miles to the Greenwich Library. The Flinn Gallery is on the second floor.

GPS Coordinates: 41.0285° N, -73.6294° W

Did You Know? The Flinn Gallery's present structure was designed by Cesar Pelli, an internationally renowned architect who also designed such famous buildings as the Petronas Towers in Kuala Lumpur, One Canada Square at Canary Wharf in London, and the Cira Centre on the Schuylkill River. He passed away in 2019.

Greenwich Avenue Historic District

In the downtown section of Greenwich, you'll find the Greenwich Avenue Historic District, with its Italianate-, Georgian Revival-, and Commercial-style buildings. This area has roots as a 1640 village that has long been a gathering place for settlers in Horseneck and Sound Beach. The area grew rapidly in the mid-19th century, becoming a wealthy community of New York City after the New Haven Railroad allowed residents to commute between Greenwich and New York City. The historic district featured merchants who provided services and goods to the booming community, and houses that were once located along Greenwich Avenue were relocated to residential districts to make room for more commercial buildings.

Best Time to Visit: To avoid crowds, visit between November and April.

Pass/Permit/Fees: There is no fee to visit the Greenwich Avenue Historic District.

Closest City or Town: Greenwich, Connecticut

How to Get There: From Hartford: Take I-91 South for 82.6 miles, then take Exit 3 onto Arch Street in Greenwich. The historic district is 0.4 miles from this exit.

GPS Coordinates: 41.0261° N, -73.6258° W

Did You Know? Buildings that should not be missed when visiting the Greenwich Avenue Historic District include the Havemeyer Building, the Greenwich Senior Center, the Main Post Office, Greenwich Town Hall, the Smith Building, the Fred Knapp Building, and St. Mary's Parish Center, among others.

Greenwich Point Park

A large sandy beach, hiking trails, and opportunities for fishing and boating make the Greenwich Point Park a popular recreational area for locals and visitors. The beach is situated on a peninsula that extends into Long Island Sound, and the waters are popular for sailing and other water sports. Two snack bars are available, but there are also grills and picnic tables if you want to have your own cookout in the park. You'll also be near the Old Greenwich Yacht Club, which is located on the west side of the point, and the Bruce Museum Seaside Center at the Innis Arden Cottage, which is open during the summer months for educational programs.

Best Time to Visit: Summer is the best time to visit Greenwich Point Park to participate in water sports and to visit the Bruce Museum Seaside Center.

Pass/Permit/Fees: A daily park pass is $8 per person.

Closest City or Town: Greenwich, Connecticut

How to Get There: From Hartford: Take I-91 South for 79.6 miles to US-1 in Greenwich. Take Exit 5 onto Sound Beach Avenue and go 2.8 miles to Tods Driftway, where you'll see the entrance to the park.

GPS Coordinates: 41.0102° N, -73.5696° W

Did You Know? The Siwanoy Indians first used the land as a fishing camp. It was known as *Monakewego* by the Siwanoys, which means "shining sands." The land was purchased in 1640 settlers for 25 coats and some other small items. Until 1944, the area was known as *Elizabeth's Neck* after Elizabeth Feake, one of the original purchasers.

Putnam Cottage

Putnam Cottage was built in the 17th century, but over the years, it has changed to reflect the attitudes and styles of the various owners. The house is generally associated with General Israel Putnam, who heroically escaped the British troops during the Revolutionary War. However, Putnam is only briefly connected to the house, since it was likely built for Timothy Knapp and his family, who lived there in the late 1600s. It was also once used as a tavern that held Freemason meetings before the Revolutionary War. In fact, the cottage was known as Knapp's Tavern during the war.

Best Time to Visit: There are no official operating hours, so be sure to call ahead to arrange your 45-minute tour. Peak season for tours is during the summer, so for a less-crowded visit, go during the fall or spring.

Pass/Permit/Fees: There is no fee to visit Putnam Cottage.

Closest City or Town: Greenwich, Connecticut

How to Get There: From the Connecticut Turnpike: Take Exit 4 (Indian Field Road) and drive for 0.7 miles to the traffic light at East Putnam Avenue. Turn left and travel for 0.7 miles through three traffic lights, and the cottage will be on the right.

GPS Coordinates: 41.0369° N, -73.6191° W

Did You Know? During the Revolutionary War, when General Putnam was residing in the house, he hosted a lunch for General George Washington and his entourage.

Montgomery Pinetum

Montgomery Pinetum is a public park surrounded by 102 acres of hiking trails through the forest. The park, which is also a historic site, is known for its rare plants and colorful wildflowers. The property was originally purchased by Colonel Robert Montgomery in 1928 and was later donated to Greenwich in 1953 following his death. Within Montgomery Pinetum, there are several rocky outcroppings that feature peaks rising up to 80 feet above sea level. Additional features of the park include greenhouses, a pond, botanical gardens, and monoliths. It's a quiet park that sees moderate traffic, which is perfect for a day away from the city.

Best Time to Visit: The best time to visit Montgomery Pinetum is during the summer when the park is open longer (until sunset).

Pass/Permit/Fees: There is no fee to visit Montgomery Pinetum.

Closest City or Town: Greenwich, Connecticut

How to Get There: From Hartford: Take I-91 South for 79.6 miles to US-1 in Greenwich. Take Exit 5 onto US-1 and travel for 1.9 miles to Bible Street, where the park is located.

GPS Coordinates: 41.0528° N, -73.5960° W

Did You Know? The term *pinetum* refers to a collection of pine trees, which are in abundance at this park. Colonel Montgomery loved to garden and planted thousands of rare conifers on his estate, which eventually became the Montgomery Pinetum.

Greenwich Audubon Center

With the mission to protect birds and their habitats, the Greenwich Audubon Center maintains seven nature sanctuaries that total 686 acres. The center is a chapter of Audubon Connecticut, which in turn is a state office of the National Audubon Society. The seven sanctuaries in Greenwich include the Main Sanctuary, the Fairchild Wildflower Audubon Sanctuary, the Gimbel Audubon Sanctuary, the Hemlock Gorge Audubon Sanctuary, the Mildred Caldwell Audubon Sanctuary of Walden Woods, the Oneida Audubon Sanctuary, and the Wood Duck Swamp Audubon Sanctuary.

Best Time to Visit: Spring and summer are the best times to visit the Greenwich Audubon Center. It's open all week between the hours of 9:00 a.m. and 5:00 p.m.

Pass/Permit/Fees: There is no fee to visit the Greenwich Audubon Center. If you participate in the programs, a $6 donation is requested.

Closest City or Town: Greenwich, Connecticut

How to Get There: From the north or south: Take I-95 to Exit 3 and turn right onto Arch Street. Turn left onto Sound View Drive. At the end of the street, turn right onto Field Point Road, then left onto Brookside Drive. At the end of this street, turn left onto Glenville Road. Drive for 1.5 miles to Riversville Road and turn right. Drive 4.5 miles to John Street, where the center will be on your right.

GPS Coordinates: 41.0970° N, -73.6879° W

Did You Know? There are 7 miles of trails that lead through old fields and hardwood forests.

Bruce Park

Four contractors, four artisans, and numerous volunteers from the Junior League of Greenwich teamed up to create a space that would provide playground opportunities to children with autism and physical disabilities. Bruce Park has four areas in which children can play. They include The Enchanted Forest, The Native American Village, a climbing area, and a play area for children ages 5 to 12. There are boulders, logs, tree stumps, a dugout canoe, and a wide variety of climbing, sliding, and pulling activities available for active kids.

Best Time to Visit: The best times to visit this park are spring, summer, and fall so that children can enjoy the facilities in warm weather.

Pass/Permit/Fees: There is no fee to visit Bruce Park.

Closest City or Town: Greenwich, Connecticut

How to Get There: From Hartford: Take I-91 South for 79.3 miles to Indian Field Road in Greenwich. Take Exit 4 onto Indian Field Road. Travel 0.5 miles to Bruce Park Drive, where the park is located.

GPS Coordinates: 41.1228° N, -73.3636° W

Did You Know? Bruce Park is located across from Bruce Museum, which showcases art, science, and natural history. Many families visit the museum first, then let their children get their energy out at Bruce Park without having to drive to a new location.

Bush-Holley House

The Bush-Holley House, a colonial saltbox structure situated at the intersection of a river and a mill pond, was built in stages beginning in 1728. It started as a one-room, two-story building that overlooked the harbor. Justus Bush purchased the house in 1738, but never lived in it. His son, David Bush, inherited the house following his father's death and significantly renovated the house in the Georgian style. He connected the original building and the house, then installed wood paneling in the parlor. It became a boarding house in 1882 when Josephine and Edward Holley opened their home to artists and writers.

Best Time to Visit: The summer is the best time to visit the Bush-Holley House, but in the fall, it will be surrounded by trees with colorful leaves. The museum store is open weekdays from 9:00 a.m. to 5:00 p.m. and 12:00 p.m. to 4:00 p.m. on Saturday and Sunday. Tours are by appointment only.

Pass/Permit/Fees: Adults ages 18 and over are $10. Seniors and students are $8. Children under the age of 18 are free.

Closest City or Town: Cos Cob, Connecticut

How to Get There: From the north or south: Take I-95 to Exit 4 and continue onto Sound Shore Drive. At the end of Sound Shore Drive, turn right onto Strickland Road and the parking lot will be on the left under the I-95 overpass.

GPS Coordinates: 41.0338° N, -73.5979° W

Did You Know? The Bush-Holley House was home to the Cos Cob Art Colony, the first one in Connecticut.

Cove Island Park

This 83-acre park is a designated recreational area located on the Long Island Sound that features hiking trails, beaches, a playground, and a cycling path just for bikes and roller blades. In the winter, the Terry Conners Ice Rink is nearby. People can enjoy ice skating or lessons when it's too cold out to explore the park. The park is home to Stamford's September 11th Memorial and SoundWaters, a facility that includes a small aquarium and various activities aboard an 80-foot schooner. According to the Audubon Society, Cove Island Park is a sanctuary for more than 280 species of birds and 50 species of butterflies.

Best Time to Visit: The park itself is best visited in the spring and summer to enjoy the hiking and swimming activities, but for ice skating, it's best visited in the winter.

Pass/Permit/Fees: A season pass is $25 for residents is $25 and $110 for non-residents.

Closest City or Town: Stamford, Connecticut

How to Get There: From Harford: Take I-91 South for 73.8 miles to US-1 North/East Main Street in Stamford. Take Exit 9 onto Weed Avenue. Travel 1.2 miles to the park's entrance.

GPS Coordinates: 41.0473° N, 73.5017° W

Did You Know? In the late 1700s, Cove Island detached from the mainland when owners expanded a flour watermill in the area. Later, it was home to the Stamford Manufacturing Company, which produced bleached minerals, licorice, and dye extracts. It burned down in 1919.

Cummings Park

Another park located on the Long Island Sound, the 79-acre Cummings Park features a boardwalk, a beach, pavilions, a snack bar, and a fishing pier. You'll also find a playground and several sports courts and fields for tennis, handball, basketball, volleyball, and softball. The Cummings Marina connects the park to West Beach, but there is a small residential neighborhood between the two areas. Anglers find the fishing pier an excellent location for yellow perch, largemouth bass, and black crappie. This park is perfect for families with children, especially those who play sports.

Best Time to Visit: Spring and summer are the best times to visit Cummings Park for its various outdoor activities.

Pass/Permit/Fees: Residents must purchase a parking pass for $25. Non-residents can purchase one for $110.

Closest City or Town: Stamford, Connecticut

How to Get There: From Hartford: Take I-91 South for 74.9 miles to Elm Street in Stamford. Take Exit 8 to Elm Street and drive 1 mile to the park's entrance.

GPS Coordinates: 41.0435° N, -73.5204° W

Did You Know? At one time, Cummings Beach was home to a seasonal harbor seal colony, but they no longer visit this beach. However, a white marble seal statue is located on the beach as a tribute to this once highly anticipated annual event.

First Presbyterian Church

Even if you don't visit First Presbyterian Church for services, it's an architectural wonder that shouldn't be missed. Built in 1958, the structure features a modern façade and carillon that resembles a fish, which is a common symbol of the Christian faith. The fish shape is seen throughout the church, both in the profile and floor plan. You'll also be amazed at the sanctuary's stained glass windows, which contain over 20,000 pieces of colored glass that tell the story of the Crucifixion and Resurrection. The 32-foot cross, also located in the sanctuary, is constructed from wood from the Canterbury Cathedral in England.

Best Time to Visit: Sunday worship is at 10:00 a.m., but if you want to tour the church, contact the church directly for tour hours.

Pass/Permit/Fees: There is no fee to visit the First Presbyterian Church.

Closest City or Town: Stamford, Connecticut

How to Get There: From Hartford: Take I-91 South for 77 miles to Elm Street in Stamford. Take Exit 8 onto Grove Street and drive for 1 mile, where you'll see the church.

GPS Coordinates: 41.0629° N, -73.5386° W

Did You Know? The church's stone wall displays several tablets that commemorate significant religious events, individuals, and institutions that impacted the community between 1641 and 1975. There is also a memorial walk from Fellowship Hall to the sanctuary that represents over 100 Judeo-Christian leaders from Abraham to today.

Half Full Brewery

Whether you're in the mood for a beer, a coffee, or a quiet space to complete some virtual work, the Half Full Brewery can accommodate your needs. This multi-use space features a coffee shop, brewery, tasting room, event space, and coworking space, complete with phone booths for private calls and adequate room to spread out your laptop. Coffees and espresso drinks are provided by Turning Point Roasters and Half Full Coffees, and all beers are brewed onsite, including Winter's Sky, Westover, Roxbury, Mango Supernova, and many more.

Best Time to Visit: The coffee shop is open from 7:00 a.m. to 2:00 p.m., the tasting room is open from 12:00 p.m. to 9:00 p.m. (10:00 p.m. on Friday and Saturday), and the beer store is open Monday through Friday from 12:00 p.m. to 9:00 p.m.

Pass/Permit/Fees: There is no fee to visit Half Full Brewery, but there are costs to purchase coffee or beer.

Closest City or Town: Stamford, Connecticut

How to Get There: From Hartford: Take I-91 South for 78.5 miles to Grenhart Road in Stamford. Take Exit 6 onto West Avenue and drive 0.9 miles to the brewery.

GPS Coordinates: 41.0394° N, -73.5501° W

Did You Know? Half Full Brewery is a purpose-driven venture with the mission of leading and inspiring the community through the production of local products and embracing the challenge to live in the moment. This was the genesis of the coffee bar-brewery-coworking space concept.

Fort Stamford Park

The gorgeous gardens at Fort Stamford Park are lovingly cared for by the Stamford Garden Club, and it is an incredible location for photographers. You'll also get your daily dose of history at this park, where you'll learn about Fort Stamford's importance during the Revolutionary War. The fort was constructed in 1781. It was near the water, yet far enough from British-controlled land to be a safe during construction. The fort allowed Stamford and the surrounding are to be secured during the war.

Best Time to Visit: The gardens are in bloom from spring until mid-summer, making these months the best time to visit.

Pass/Permit/Fees: There is no fee to visit Fort Stamford Park.

Closest City or Town: Stamford, Connecticut

How to Get There: From Hartford: Take I-91 South for 73.8 miles to Den Road in Stamford. Take Exit 33 and go 1.7 miles to Westover Road and the park's entrance.

GPS Coordinates: 41.0847° N, -73.5790° W

Did You Know? Even though Fort Stamford was viewed as surplus property after the war, and the land was promptly sold, you can still see the redoubts built by the soldiers at each corner of the garrison. A stone marker indicates the former location of the main fort and was dedicated by the Stamford chapter of the Daughters of the American Revolution in 1926. To the west of the formal garden, there is a 250-year-old tree still standing that was alive during the Revolutionary War.

Stamford Museum & Nature Center

Dedicated to the preservation of art, popular culture, history, natural sciences, and agricultural sciences, the Stamford Museum & Nature Center is a place where art and nature become the focal point for lifelong learning and exploration. A visit to the museum will take you through the Knobloch Family Farmhouse, which allows for experiential learning even during the cold months of the year. You'll also see Heckscher Farm, the Overbrook Nature Center, the Observatory & Planetarium, the Edith & Robert Graham Otter Pond, and Bendel Mansion.

Best Time to Visit: Though you can visit at any time of year because of the Knobloch Family Farmhouse, the best times to visit are spring and summer so that you can see more of the grounds.

Pass/Permit/Fees: Adult admission is $14, and children between the ages of 4 and 17 are $8. Students are $10 and seniors are $12. Children ages 3 and under are free.

Closest City or Town: Stamford, Connecticut

How to Get There: From Hartford: Take I-91 South for 72.4 miles to High Ridge Road in Stamford. Take Exit 35 onto High Ridge Road and follow it 1.1 miles to the museum.

GPS Coordinates: 41.1261° N, -73.5457° W

Did You Know? The Stamford Museum & Nature Center is host to various events throughout the year, including drive-in movie nights, concerts, and special exhibitions.

Stamford Observatory

Located at the Stamford Museum & Nature Center, the Stamford Planetarium & Observatory allows visitors to explore the night sky, either on the dome of the planetarium or through the 22-inch research telescope in the observatory. Viewers will be treated to live views of the moon, other planets, and various deep space objects. On certain Friday nights, you can visit the Knobloch Family Farmhouse to enjoy a presentation on topics related to space. Attendees can then catch a glimpse of the stars through telescopes.

Best Time to Visit: Contact the Planetarium & Observatory directly for times and observatory availability. Since this attraction is outside most of the time, spring and summer are the best times to visit.

Pass/Permit/Fees: Adult admission to the observatory is $5, and children are priced at $3.

Closest City or Town: Stamford, Connecticut

How to Get There: From Hartford: Take I-91 South for 72.4 miles to High Ridge Road in Stamford. Take Exit 35 onto High Ridge Road and follow it 1.1 miles to the museum.

GPS Coordinates: 41.1244° N, -73.5491° W

Did You Know? The primary use of the observatory is as a research tool for members of the Fairfield County Astronomical Society. It may not be open to the public on the day of your visit, so be sure to call ahead to make sure you'll be able to use the telescope.

The Ferguson Library

Built in 1880, The Ferguson Library has long had the mission to make books, recordings, films, and other materials available to the public. Additionally, the library is a center of literacy for people of all ages, and the innovative programs and services provided by the library encourage a life-long love of learning. Not only is there an extensive children's program, which is the staple of many libraries, but there are also events specific to adults and teens, making this library a truly integral part of the local community. The library has been free to the public since 1911, following the library's belief that knowledge should be available to everyone.

Best Time to Visit: The library is open year round and is a wonderful place to visit during any month. It is open from 10:00 a.m. to at least 5:00 p.m. every day except Sunday, when it doesn't open until 1:00 p.m.

Pass/Permit/Fees: There is no fee to visit the Ferguson Library.

Closest City or Town: Stamford, Connecticut

How to Get There: From the north: Take I-95 South to Exit 8 (Elm Street). At the third light on Elm Street, turn right onto Atlantic Street. After five lights, you will see the library ahead at the corner of Broad and Bedford streets.

GPS Coordinates: 41.0556° N, -73.5392° W

Did You Know? The library is named for John Day Ferguson, who moved to Stamford in 1842. Upon his death in 1877, he left $10,000 to build a library to further the education of the public.

Mianus River Park

A family-oriented gem located in Stamford, the Mianus River Park is a 391-acre nature reserve that features a two-mile stretch of the Mianus River. While the river is the main attraction to park guests, there are also miles of hiking trails throughout the park, vernal pools, and the opportunity to see various wildlife. The Mianus River is a main source of drinking water for more than 100,000 people living in Greenwich, Stamford, and nearby New York communities. Birdwatching, cross country skiing, fishing, hiking, and geocaching are all popular activities in the park.

Best Time to Visit: The summer is the best time to visit Mianus River Park to enjoy the water. The weather will be cooler in the spring and fall for hikes and other activities.

Pass/Permit/Fees: There is no fee to visit Mianus River Park.

Closest City or Town: Stamford, Connecticut

How to Get There: From Hartford: Take I-91 South for 73.8 miles to Den Road in Stamford. Take Exit 33, then take Westover Road for 2 miles to Merriebrook Lane, where the park is located.

GPS Coordinates: 41.08184° N, -73.58044° W

Did You Know? More than 150 species of resident and migratory birds can be found in Mianus River Park, 70 of which use the park for breeding grounds. Watch for heron, kingfishers, warblers, and woodpeckers, among others.

Mill River Park

This relatively small, 12-acre urban park is a popular rest stop for visitors to downtown Stamford. It features a carousel, an ice-skating rink in the winter, and various trails that connect with others in Scalzi, Southfield, and Kosciuszko parks. Mill River Park is known for its 120 cherry trees, which were given to Stamford in 1957 by Junzo Nojima, a Japanese native who settled in Stamford in 1926. Nojima, who would become the first Japanese restaurant owner in Connecticut, watered every single tree for three years until they were established. Even today, it is the largest grove of cherry trees in New England.

Best Time to Visit: The best time to visit Mill River Park is in the summer for most activities and in the winter for ice skating.

Pass/Permit/Fees: There is no fee to visit Hill River Park.

Closest City or Town: Stamford, Connecticut

How to Get There: From Hartford: Take I-91 South for 74.9 miles to Elm Street in Stamford. Take Exit 8 to Broad Street and drive 1 mile to the park's entrance.

GPS Coordinates: 41.0543° N, -73.5449° W

Did You Know? In 2007, Mill River Park underwent an $8.5 million expansion, which included the removal of the Mill River dam and the narrowing of the river's width to increase the park's square footage. This allowed the park to install more amenities, including the carousel and skating rink. The removal of the dam also allowed fish to move up from the Long Island Sound.

Bartlett Arboretum & Gardens

In 1913, Francis A. Bartlett, an internationally known dendrologist (tree scientist), purchased 30 acres near Stamford. He used the land for his home, a research lab, and a training school for his tree-care business, the F.A. Bartlett Tree Expert Company. Between then and 1965, Bartlett gathered many tree specimens on the property from locations in Asia, Europe, and the United States. When Bartlett moved to North Carolina in 1965, the State of Connecticut purchased his land and designated it as the Connecticut State Arboretum. The arboretum was opened to the public in 1966, and additional acres of land were added to enhance the property. Today, visitors can enjoy award-winning champion trees, fields of wildflowers, woodland hiking trails, varied wildlife, and much more.

Best Time to Visit: Spring is the best time to see the wildflowers, and fall is the best to see the leaves change.

Pass/Permit/Fees: There is no fee to visit the Bartlett Arboretum & Gardens except for special events.

Closest City or Town: Stamford, Connecticut

How to Get There: From north or south: Take I-95 to Exit 7, then take Route 137 (High Ridge Road) for 6.3 miles to Brookdale Road. Turn left on Brookdale Road and go 0.3 miles to the entrance.

GPS Coordinates: 41.1323° N, -73.5496° W

Did You Know? When you're hiking through the arboretum and gardens, be on the lookout for miniature sculptures of heads hidden among the rocks, trails, and trees. Check the website for clues to finding these heads.

Earthplace

Earthplace is a nonprofit organization with the mission to build passion and respect for nature through a combination of science, education, and conservation. This 62-acre nature and wildlife sanctuary provides public access to various habitats such as ponds, streams, fields, and forests. It features 2 miles of hiking trails that cross the sanctuary. There is also a water quality research laboratory on the premises that serves over 200 field sites and educational programs. A picnic grove, learning center, and outdoor amphitheater round out the attractions located at Earthplace.

Best Time to Visit: During the school year, there will be fewer crowds than during the summer or school breaks.

Pass/Permit/Fees: There is no fee to visit Earthplace if you want to hike the trails. Some attractions may require membership. Contact the facility directly to inquire about membership fees.

Closest City or Town: Westport, Connecticut

How to Get There: From I-95, take Exit 17, then turn left onto Route 33 North. Go 1.5 miles to Route 1 (Post Road). Turn left onto Route 1 and travel 0.5 miles to the second traffic light. Turn right at the light onto King's Highway North. Turn left at the first place possible onto Woodside Avenue, and travel for 0.9 miles to the entrance.

GPS Coordinates: 41.0844° N, -73.2253° W

Did You Know? Letterboxes and Word Hunting are two games that can be played while on Earthplace's trails. Download the instructions on Earthplace's website.

Compo Beach

At 29 acres in size, Compo Beach offers an extensive sand beach with access to the Long Island Sound and the Saugatuck River. The park features a boardwalk, concession stand, sand volleyball courts, a softball field, a multi-purpose field, lighted basketball courts, a skate park, an open skate area, a pavilion, a wooden playground, and easy access to the Ned Dimes Marina. Even though the beach is open all year, daily passes are limited to 100 per day to make sure the beach is enjoyable for all visitors.

Best Time to Visit: Since there is a fee to visit the beach between May and October, if you want to visit for free, the best time to visit is between November and April. However, for sports and water activities, summer is the best time to go.

Pass/Permit/Fees: The fee to visit Compo Beach between May 1 and September 30 is $45 per vehicle on weekdays and $70 per vehicle on weekends and holidays.

Closest City or Town: Westport, Connecticut

How to Get There: From Hartford: Take I-91 South for 61.2 miles to Weston Road in Westport. Take Exit 43 onto Compo Road and follow it for 4.6 miles to the park's entrance.

GPS Coordinates: 41.1063° N, -73.3523° W

Did You Know? Compo Beach is an excellent place for families with small children, as the water is waveless and calm. At low tide, you'll be able to find numerous sea creatures native to New England, including crabs, fish, and even tiny octopuses.

Westport Country Playhouse

Before it became a playhouse in 1931, the building that now houses the Westport Country Playhouse was first a tannery and then a steam-powered cider mill. By the 1920s, the building was standing empty. Lawrence Langer and his wife, Armina Marshall, were theatrical producers. They bought the barn to start their own theater close to home. Originally, it was named Woodland Theatre, but the name was changed to Country Playhouse on opening night. Since then, more than 800 theatrical productions have taken the stage at Westport Country Playhouse, including *Come Back, Little Sheba*, *Butterflies Are Free*, and *Our Town*.

Best Time to Visit: The season for plays runs from June to December, so plan your visit to include a show during these months.

Pass/Permit/Fees: The outdoor areas of the playhouse's campus are free to visit, but tickets to plays vary based on the production and where the seats are located. Contact the playhouse directly to purchase tickets.

Closest City or Town: Westport, Connecticut

How to Get There: From New Haven: Take I-95 to Exit 18 and merge right onto Sherwood Island Connector. Turn left onto Route 1 (Post Road). You will see the playhouse on the right after you pass four traffic lights.

GPS Coordinates: 41.1420° N, -73.3545° W

Did You Know? In 1940, Richard Rodgers saw *Green Grow the Lilacs* at the playhouse and was inspired to write *Oklahoma!* with Oscar Hammerstein II.

Westport Farmers' Market

As a trial run in the parking lot of Westport Country Playhouse, the Westport Farmers' Market opened its doors in June 2006. At the time, the market featured 14 vendors and saw 500 customers the first weekend. The market grew to the point where a new location was needed, and it moved to its current spot near the Saugatuck River. The market now offers much more than just fresh produce and organic options. There are now 45 vendors, and it is open even during parts of the winter. Various programs such as We Care, Friend of the Market, and Farmer in Need, among others, enhance the market's connection to its local roots.

Best Time to Visit: The Westport Farmers' Market is only open on Thursdays between May 13 and November 11.

Pass/Permit/Fees: There is no cost to visit the Westport Farmers' Market, but have money on hand to buy some of the wonderful food you'll discover there.

Closest City or Town: Westport, Connecticut

How to Get There: From Hartford: Take I-91 South for 61.2 miles to Weston Road in Westport. Take Exit 42 onto Compo Road, then travel 2.2 miles to Imperial Avenue, where you'll see the market.

GPS Coordinates: 41.1382° N, -73.3603° W

Did You Know? The Westport Farmers' Market was inspired by Paul Newman and Michel Nischan. In the winter months (late October and November), the market moves inside to Gilbertie's Herb Garden, located at 7 Sylvan Lane.

Westport Museum for History and Culture

The mission of Westport Museum for History and Culture is to preserve, present, and celebrate Westport history since its inception in 1889. An interactive museum that contains games, art, recreation, and a gift shop, the center also provides history-related events. Additionally, the museum restored and maintains the Adams Academy, an authentic one-room schoolhouse that operated in Westport from 1837 to 1867. The house that contains the museum was built in 1795, and its remodeling in the 19th century is an architectural example of the Italianate Style popular at that time.

Best Time to Visit: Since the museum is closed on Sunday and Monday, plan your visit for Tuesday through Friday between the hours of 11:00 a.m. and 5:00 p.m. On Saturday, it is only open until 4:00 p.m.

Pass/Permit/Fees: There is no fee to visit the Westport Museum for History and Culture.

Closest City or Town: Westport, Connecticut

How to Get There: From I-95: Take Exit 17 and turn left onto Route 33. Take Route 33 to Route 1 and turn right. Take Route 1 (Post Road) to Main Street and turn left. Then, turn right on Avery Place, where you'll see the museum.

GPS Coordinates: 41.1446° N, -73.3610° W

Did You Know? The Cobblestone Barn is the only one in Connecticut to have an eight-sided roof.

Westport Paddle Club

Located at Bridgebrook Marina, the Westport Paddle Club provides paddle board and kayak lessons and tours. It even offers a summer camp for children ages 7 and up who want to explore the Saugatuck River on a stand-up paddle board or in a kayak. The club's mission is to increase ocean awareness and help visitors develop their paddling skills. In addition to becoming more confident in paddling, visitors will also learn boating rules, equipment care, and ocean safety.

Best Time to Visit: Summer is the best time to visit the Westport Paddle Club. It is open Monday through Sunday from 9:00 a.m. to 6:00 p.m. and by appointment.

Pass/Permit/Fees: There is no fee to visit the Westport Paddle Club, but paddle boat and kayak rentals do have a fee. One-hour paddle board or kayak rentals are $35, and two-hour paddle board or kayak rentals are $50.

Closest City or Town: Westport, Connecticut

How to Get There: From Hartford: Take I-91 South for 65.2 miles to Saugatuck Avenue in Westport. Take Exit 17 onto Saugatuck Avenue, then travel 0.3 miles to Riverside Avenue, where the club is located.

GPS Coordinates: 41.1245° N, -73.3717° W

Did You Know? Jewell, founder of Westport Paddle Club, was an instructor at the Riverside Avenue Downunder kayak and paddle boarding shop until it closed in 2019. The day before it closed, the owner of Bridgebrook Marina suggested Jewell start a similar business there, and the Westport Paddle Club was born.

Levitt Pavilion for the Performing Arts

The Levitt Pavilion is home to outdoor festivals, concerts, and other performing arts productions. In the past four decades of the pavilion's existence, the feature production has been 50 Free Nights Under the Stars, which presents a different musical guest each night. More than 1.5 million guests have attended these free concerts. The mission of the Levitt Pavilion for the Performing Arts is to ensure citizens have "free and abundant access to the performing arts." It also seeks to provide support to diverse artists from all over the world by giving them a venue to perform.

Best Time to Visit: Summer is the best time to visit the Levitt Pavilion for the Performing Arts, as the majority of its shows are scheduled for the warmer months of the year.

Pass/Permit/Fees: There is no fee to attend any of the events at the Levitt Pavilion for the Performing Arts.

Closest City or Town: Westport, Connecticut

How to Get There: From Hartford: Take I-91 South for 61.2 miles to Weston Road in Westport. Take Exit 42 onto Main Street and continue 2 miles to the pavilion.

GPS Coordinates: 41.1382° N, -73.3617° W

Did You Know? RiverSwing is held on several evenings throughout the summer during which guests can get free pre-concert dance lessons from professionals. The style of dance they will learn is the same style they will be listening to during the concert.

Longshore Park

This municipal par-69 golf course is rated as the eighth best place to play a round of golf in Connecticut. The course was designed and constructed in the mid 1920s by Orin E. Smith, but was eventually renovated by architect John Harvey. Before becoming the premier golf course in Fairfield County, Longshore Park was an onion farm. Once a golfer is done with their 18 holes, they can relax in a famous and award-winning lodge: The Inn at Longshore. This idyllic lodge features 12 rooms, all modernly decorated to ensure a comfortable and memorable stay.

Best Time to Visit: Spring and fall provide the best golfing weather in Connecticut, but summer is popular as well, especially in the mornings.

Pass/Permit/Fees: Golfing rates at Longshore Park begin at $26 for 9 holes and $31 for 18 holes for a resident. The cost for non-residents is $39 for 9 holes and $52 for 18 holes.

Closest City or Town: Westport, Connecticut

How to Get There: From Hartford: Take I-91 South for 61.2 miles to Weston Road in Westport. Take Exit 42 onto Compo Road, then travel for 4.3 miles to Old Cuttings Lane.

GPS Coordinates: 41.1117° N, -73.3635° W

Did You Know? The restaurant at The Inn at Longshore is a popular place to sip on cocktails or enjoy full seafood meals. One of the largest waterfront event locations in the county, it can also be booked for private events.

MoCA Westport

This museum is dedicated to presenting diverse and innovative visual and performing art from emerging, established, and local artists. One of its most popular presentations is its concert series that features well-known musicians in various genres. There are also numerous educational opportunities for children, teens, and adults in the creative arts that allow them to interact with materials in meaningful ways. Lectures, family art days, and artist talks represent just some of the programming available at MoCA Westport that is designed to engage audiences and inspire artistic expression.

Best Time to Visit: The gallery is open Wednesday through Sunday between the hours of 12:00 p.m. and 4:00 p.m., and the academy is open Monday through Friday between 9:00 a.m. and 3:45 p.m.

Pass/Permit/Fees: General admission for visitors ages 13 and up is $10. Children ages 12 and under are free. Students, educators, and seniors over the age of 60 are $5.

Closest City or Town: Westport, Connecticut

How to Get There: From Hartford: Take I-91 South for 62.2 miles to Westport, then take Exit 41 onto the Newtown Turnpike. Continue 1 mile to the museum.

GPS Coordinates: 40.7418° N, -73.9893° W

Did You Know? Until 2019, the MoCA Westport was known as the Westport Arts Center, but the name was changed to reflect the center's new mission.

Sherwood Island State Park

Connecticut's first state park, Sherwood Island, is 235 acres of recreational space located in the Greens Farms area of Westport. Thomas Sherwood arrived in the 1600s and settled on Fox Island, which was then a separate section of land that ran through what is now the park. He acquired a gristmill on Mill Pond. Throughout the 1800s, Sherwood's descendants grew onions, potatoes, and other crops on what became known as Sherwood Island. Local farmers used the gristmill for many years until grain farming declined in Connecticut.

Best Time to Visit: Fishing in Sherwood Island State Park is best in the spring, but the views are best in the fall when the leaves are changing colors.

Pass/Permit/Fees: There is no fee for residents to visit Sherwood Island State Park, but non-residents are charged $22 per vehicle on weekends and holidays, and $15 on weekdays. After 4:00 p.m., there is a $7 per vehicle charge.

Closest City or Town: Green Farms, Connecticut

How to Get There: From I-95 north and south: Take I-95 to Exit 18 to access the Sherwood Island Connector. The connector will take you directly into the park.

GPS Coordinates: 41.1155° N, -73.3331° W

Did You Know? Although the park was purchased by the Connecticut State Park Commission in 1914, making it officially the first state park in Connecticut, it wasn't open to the public until after 1937 because several parcel owners in the area objected to the development.

Lake Mohegan

Just off Morehouse Highway, you'll find the 170.4-acre Lake Mohegan. This manmade freshwater lake is popular with swimmers, especially because there are lifeguards on duty. The sandy beach is large, but has little shade, so be sure to bring an umbrella. A sprinkler park is available on the property, along with a playground, picnic shelter, restrooms, and a snack bar. Children can even take swimming lessons in the lake starting at age 4.

Best Time to Visit: The lake and sprinkler park are open between Memorial Day and Labor Day, so if you plan to swim, these are the months to visit. However, the open space around the lake is open year round.

Pass/Permit/Fees: On weekdays, adult residents are $8 each, and children between the ages of 3 and 17 are $4 each. Adult non-residents are $15 each and children are $8 each. On weekends, adult residents are $10 each and children are $6 each. Adult non-residents are $18 each and children are $12 each.

Closest City or Town: Fairfield, Connecticut

How to Get There: From Hartford: Take I-91 South and Connecticut Highway 15 South for 54.2 miles to Congress Street. Take Exit 46 onto Congress Street. Travel 1.4 miles to Morehouse Highway, where you'll see the lake's entrance.

GPS Coordinates: 41.20293° N, -73.25342° W

Did You Know? While fishing is only allowed from the shoreline on Lake Mohegan, anglers find it a popular place to catch trout.

Trout Brook Valley State Park

Trout Brook Valley State Park is a 300-acre reserve that makes up a portion of the 758-acre preservation effort across the towns of Weston and Easton. It's a walk-in-only park that is crisscrossed with dirt roads. Enjoy the views of the coniferous and deciduous forest, and watch for wildlife, water sources, and wetlands. There are many trails to explore in the park, with the loop running from the Green Trail to the Red Trail to the White Trail being the most popular. Other fun trails include the loop that connects Crow Hill Preserve Pink Trail to the Blue and White trails, Pop Mountain, and the Red Trail.

Best Time to Visit: The fall is the best time to visit Trout Brook Valley State Park if you want to hike through the gorgeous forest as the leaves are changing colors.

Pass/Permit/Fees: There is no fee to visit Trout Brook Valley State Park.

Closest City or Town: Easton, Connecticut

How to Get There:
From Hartford: Take I-91 South from Whitehead Highway for 55.6 miles to Congress Street in Fairfield. Take Exit 44 onto Connecticut Highway 58 North. Take Connecticut 58 North for 6.5 miles to Bradley Hill Road. There is limited parking on Bradley Road near the reserve.

GPS Coordinates: 41.24619° N, -73.34251° W

Did You Know? Trout Brook Valley State Park was set to be sold to developers in 1999 when it was saved by Aspetuck Land Trust and support from citizens, including actor Paul Newman and his daughter Lissy Newman.

Twin Brooks Park

Dedicated as Trumbull, Connecticut's "Ecology Park," Twin Brooks Park has been transformed from a gravel supply location to a natural swimming area. There are many scenic overlooks in the park, and it is contiguous with Beach Memorial Park, a woodland area that features many miles of nature trails. In addition to the swimming area, visitors can enjoy nature ponds, a picnic area, wildflower fields, a multi-purpose field, a playground, and in the winter, an ice-skating rink and a sledding hill.

Best Time to Visit: The best time to visit the swimming area in Twin Brooks Park is in the summer, when you'll want to cool off from the heat. However, the ice-skating rink and sledding hills make this a great place to visit in the winter as well.

Pass/Permit/Fees: Residents with must have a parking permit. Currently, non-residents are not able to get a parking permit at this time. You will need to park away and take public transportation or walk in. Violations cost $25.

Closest City or Town: Trumbull, Connecticut

How to Get There: From Hartford: Take I-91 South from Whitehead Highway for 50 miles to Connecticut Highway 127 North/White Plains Road in Trumbull. Take Exit 50 onto Twitchgrass Road. Follow the road for 1.1 miles to Twin Brooks Drive to arrive at the park.

GPS Coordinates: 41.2451° N, -73.1862° W

Did You Know? There is a 2.5-mile hiking loop around the park that is appropriate for all skill levels.

Indian Well State Park

The waterfalls at this park, one of which is 15 feet tall, are the main attraction. On the western bank of the Housatonic River, there is a shady picnic area along the water's edge. Swimming in the splash pool is allowed, along with fishing and kayaking. The park encompasses 150 acres and is the home of the New Haven Rowing Club, which holds annual regattas at the park. Fishing in the river is also a popular activity, and anglers can expect to catch carp, white catfish, bass, perch, American eel, and sunfish.

Best Time to Visit: The park is open year round, but is best visited between April and November. The falls will be more spectacular in the spring, while the colorful foliage will make a fall visit worthwhile.

Pass/Permit/Fees: There is no fee for residents to visit Indian Well State Park, but non-residents will be charged $15 per vehicle on weekends and holidays, and $10 per vehicle on weekdays. Visits after 4:00 p.m. are $6 per vehicle.

Closest City or Town: Shelton, Connecticut

How to Get There: From Hartford: Take I-84 for 47.4 miles to Connecticut Highway 110 North/Howe Avenue in Shelton. Take Exit 14 onto Connecticut 110 North to Indian Well Road, where you'll see the park's entrance.

GPS Coordinates: 41.34383° N, -73.12651° W

Did You Know? Indian Well State Park gets its name from a Native American legend about two star-crossed lovers who died near the falls in a similar way to Romeo and Juliet.

Palace Theatre

Over 90 years of history is found in the Palace Theatre, which was the center of the cultural scene in Connecticut from when it was built in the 1920s to just before World War II. The architecture is a blend of Roman, Arabic, Greek, and Federal styles. It was designed by period architect Thomas Lamb. Originally, the theater was a movie house that also presented vaudeville shows, but it evolved into whatever was needed during specific periods in the 20th century. For example, silent films were shown at the theater, and it was the location of many big band and rock concerts as well. Following a $30 million renovation in the 1990s, the theater became a premier theatrical facility for live theater.

Best Time to Visit: The theater's season runs from October to June each year, so if you want to see a show, that's the time to visit. Specific dates (one per month) for tours are listed on the website.

Pass/Permit/Fees: There is no fee to tour the theater, but if you decide to see a show, rates will vary.

Closest City or Town: Waterbury, Connecticut

How to Get There: From Hartford: Take I-84 for 28.6 miles to Brass Mill Drive in Waterbury. Take Exit 22 and drive 0.6 miles to Main Street, where the theater is located.

GPS Coordinates: 41.5552° N, -73.0392° W

Did You Know? Between 2004 and 2014, the theater served more than 1 million guests at plays, musicals, and other performing art productions.

Mirror Lake

Mirror Lake, also known as Hubbard Park Pond, is located in Hubbard Park in Meriden. This extremely smooth, glossy lake offers a jaw-dropping view during the fall. The foliage colors from the surrounding trees are reflected in the water, thereby giving the lake its name. In the winter, when the water freezes over, Mirror Lake is a popular location for ice skating. The lake is the southern tip of the Merimere Reservoir and features an exposure of sandstone and basalt from two major lava flows that once covered the Meriden valley. You'll clearly see a two-foot layer of sandstone that covers red clay and basalt from early volcanic activity.

Best Time to Visit: In the fall, you'll get postcard images of the famed New England foliage, and in the winter, you can skate on the frozen surface of the lake.

Pass/Permit/Fees: There is no fee to visit Mirror Lake, but there will be a fee to ice skate in the winter.

Closest City or Town: Meriden, Connecticut

How to Get There: From Middletown: Take I-91 to Cromwell, then take I-691 West to Exit 4. Turn left on Southington/Route 322. Continue on West Main Street, where you'll see Hubbard Park on the left about a mile from the exit.

GPS Coordinates: 41.54799° N, -72.83509° W

Did You Know? Fishing is popular at Mirror Lake, and it's possible to catch a variety of species, including bluegill, bullhead, largemouth bass, yellow perch, calico bass, and trout.

Chauncey Peak Trail

This 3-mile trail in Giuffrida Park is rated as easy to moderate and is appropriate for most skill levels. The park is 600 acres in size and encompasses Crescent Lake. The trail will take hikers to the 688-foot Chauncey Peak, a traprock mountain contained within the Metacomet Ridge. The views from the summit are breathtaking, with scenic vistas that overlook Crescent Lake. As the initial ascent was rather steep, a 2017 reroute was required to make it more gradual for inexperienced hikers. The trail's descent is now the most challenging part of this hike and should be attempted with care. Additionally, some parts of the trail skirt the cliff's edge, so take extra precautions when hiking these areas.

Best Time to Visit: Summer and fall are the best times to visit to avoid wet areas on the trail, which can become slippery and somewhat dangerous.

Pass/Permit/Fees: There is no fee to hike Chauncey Peak Trail.

Closest City or Town: Meriden, Connecticut

How to Get There: From Hartford: Take I-91 South for 14.4 miles to Middle Street in Middletown. Take Exit 20 onto Country Club Road. Follow Country Club Road for 2.3 miles to Westfield Road and the trailhead in Meriden.

GPS Coordinates: 41.5584° N, -72.7595° W

Did You Know? The park that contains Chauncey Peak Trail is named for Dr. Francis Giuffrida, a surgeon who lived in Meriden and served in the U.S. Navy and Marine Corps from 1941 to 1946, in both the Atlantic and Pacific.

Mattabesett Blue Trail

If you're looking for a longer day hike, try the Mattabesett Blue Trail, a 10.4-mile hiking path for moderately skilled hikers. You can walk or bike on this trail, and dogs are allowed as long as they are leashed. On the way, you will get some spectacular views of Middletown, Wallingford, and the Connecticut River. While there are some steep sections, it's mostly a gentle incline on a well-marked path. The Mattabesett Blue Trail is part of a 62-mile-long system that winds through the state and is one of the first trails that was developed by early Connecticut hikers. Be aware that it is very popular and likely to be crowded on weekends and holidays. Look for the Chinese Wall feature as you pass through Middletown.

Best Time to Visit: The best time to visit the Mattabesett Blue Trail is spring when the wildflowers are in bloom.

Pass/Permit/Fees: There is no fee to visit the Mattabesett Blue Trail.

Closest City or Town: Middlefield, Connecticut

How to Get There: From Hartford: Take I-91 from Whitehead Highway for 16.2 miles to Connecticut Highway 17 in Middletown. Take Exit 13 onto Connecticut 17 and follow it 9.6 miles to the trailhead.

GPS Coordinates: 41.40909° N, -72.69640° W

Did You Know? *Mattabesett* is the Indian word for Middletown.

Sleeping Giant State Park

This state park gets its name from 2 miles of mountain top that look like a huge man sleeping. There is a 1.5-mile trail that leads to a stone observation tower at the top of Mount Carmel, where you can get a spectacular view of the Long Island Sound. Fishing is available in the stream that flows through the park, and it is a designated Trout Management Area, so be sure to know the rules before you drop your line.

Best Time to Visit: The best times to visit Sleeping Giant State Park are summer for the warm temperatures and fall to see the gorgeous leaf colors.

Pass/Permit/Fees: For residents, there is no charge to visit Sleeping Giant State Park. For non-residents, it is $15 per vehicle on weekends and holidays, and $10 per vehicle on weekdays.

Closest City or Town: Hamden, Connecticut

How to Get There: From I-91: Take Exit 10 to the Route 40 connector and remain on this road until it ends. At the light, turn right onto Route 10 North and drive 1.5 miles to Mount Carmel Avenue. Turn right onto Mount Carmel Avenue and drive to the park entrance, which will be on your left across from Quinnipiac University.

GPS Coordinates: 41.4304° N, -72.8870° W

Did You Know? You'll be able to see distinct features of the sleeping giant, including a head, chin, chest, hip, knee, and feet. If you look closely, you'll be able to see scars on the giant's head that were left there from a rock quarry that closed in 1933.

Silver Sands State Park

This 297-acre recreation area provides visitors with an area to swim, picnic, hike, or bird watch. When the tide is low and the sandbar (called the *tombolo*) is visible, you can walk to Charles Island, where there is a bird sanctuary. If you decide to do this, make sure to watch the tides as you will be unable to cross during high tide. Crossing to Charles Island is not permissible between May 1 and September 9 as there are nesting birds on the island.

Best Time to Visit: While the park is open year round, if you want to visit Charles Island, you will need to visit between September 10 and April 30.

Pass/Permit/Fees: There is no fee for residents to visit Silver Sands State Park, but non-residents are charged $15 per vehicle on weekends and holidays, and $10 per vehicle on weekends. After 4:00 p.m., non-residents are charged $6 per vehicle.

Closest City or Town: Milford, Connecticut

How to Get There: From I-95: Take Exit 35 south onto Schoolhouse Road to Route 1 (Bridgeport Avenue). Turn left onto Route 1 and head towards Silver Sands Park Way (the first light). Take Silver Sands Park Way past Meadowside Road to the park's entrance.

GPS Coordinates: 41.20054° N, -73.06766° W

Did You Know? When the tide comes in, the tombolo between the beach and Charles Island will be completely submerged, and you will not be able to return to the park until it goes out again. **Do not walk on any part of the tombolo when it is under water**.

Charles Island

This 14-acre island is located in the Long Island Sound off the coast of Milford. It is viewable from the beach at Silver Sands State Park. It is accessible by foot when the tide is low, and visitors can see the sandbar (tombolo) between the beach and island. Currently, there are about two hours twice a day when pedestrians can safely cross the tombolo, but as erosion continues to shrink the size of the sandbar, the crossing windows become smaller. Nesting birds on Charles Island are protected from visitors between May 1 and September 9, which means no one can cross to the island during those dates.

Best Time to Visit: While you can see Charles Island from Silver Sands State Park all year long, you will only be able to cross over between September 10 and April 30.

Pass/Permit/Fees: There is no fee to visit Charles Island, but non-residents will pay $15 per vehicle to park at Silver Sands State Park on weekends and holidays, and $10 per vehicle on weekdays. After 4:00 p.m., the rate drops to $6 per vehicle.

Closest City or Town: Milford, Connecticut

How to Get There: From I-95: Take Exit 35 south onto Schoolhouse Road to Route 1 (Bridgeport Avenue). Turn left onto Route 1 to Silver Sands Park Way (the first light). Take Silver Sands Park Way past Meadowside Road to the park's entrance.

GPS Coordinates: 41.19140° N, -73.0583° W

Did You Know? There is a legend that Captain Kid buried his treasure on Charles Island in 1699.

East Rock Park

Formed approximately 200 million years ago when the continental plates were spreading apart and molten lava flowed through the resulting cracks, East Rock, for which East Rock Park is named, rose more than 350 feet above the Mill River Valley below. The prominence of this park provides superior views of the Long Island Sound, and the nature trails within its boundaries offer various vantage points of the harbor. This park is also a bird sanctuary, offering 427 acres of safety from predators, development, and other perils. There are various sports fields and courts at the base of the mountain. Snowshoeing and cross-country skiing are popular in the winter.

Best Time to Visit: East Rock Park is open year round, so spring and summer visits are ideal for warm-weather sports. Winter is the perfect time to visit for snow sports.

Pass/Permit/Fees: There is no fee to visit East Rock Park.

Closest City or Town: New Haven, Connecticut

How to Get There: From Hartford: Take I-91 South for 29.4 miles to Hartford Turnpike in North Haven. Take Exit 63 onto Hartford Turnpike, then travel for 5.2 miles to the park.

GPS Coordinates: 41.3296° N, -72.9046° W

Did You Know? The Trowbridge Environmental Center is located in the park and provides educational information about the area's geology and ecosystem. It is open Thursdays and Fridays from 10:00 a.m. to 5:00 p.m.

Ely Center of Contemporary Art

The Ely Center of Contemporary Art is located in the historic John Slade Ely House in New Haven. The nonprofit organization formed when Wells Fargo attempted to sell the house and turn it into grant-making trust rather than an operational art center. The sale was successfully blocked, and the house continues to present modern art exhibits and educational events to engage the community in all kinds of art.

Best Time to Visit: The museum is only open on Sunday and Monday from 1:00 p.m. to 4:00 p.m., and Thursday from 3:00 p.m. to 8:00 p.m. With these limited hours, a visit to this attraction will need to be carefully planned. Additionally, you may contact the museum through the website to request a private appointment.

Pass/Permit/Fees: There is no fee to visit the Ely Center of Contemporary Art, but the curators do accept donations.

Closest City or Town: New Haven, Connecticut

How to Get There: From Hartford: Take I-91 South for 37 miles to Trumbull Street in New Haven. Take Exit 3 and the center will be on the right.

GPS Coordinates: 41.3128° N, -72.9204° W

Did You Know? The John Slade Ely House is a gorgeous Elizabethan-era mansion that was constructed in 1901. Both John Slade Ely and his wife, Grace Taylor Ely, were active members of the New Haven arts community until their deaths in 1906 and 1959, respectively.

Carousel at Lighthouse Point Park

The historic Lighthouse Point Park Carousel is one of fewer than 100 such carousels in operation in the U.S. today. At one point in the 1920s, there were 10,000 carousels across the country, but they have gradually disappeared over time. This carousel was built in 1916 and is now considered a rare representation of American folk art. However, due to exposure to the elements along the ocean, the carousel was dismantled in 1977, only to be unearthed again three years later by a group that would restore the carousel and return it to the pavilion in 1983.

Best Time to Visit: Summer is the best time to visit the carousel at Lighthouse Park and get incredible views of the Long Island Sound and New Haven Harbor. Try to visit in the afternoon and stay until sunset.

Pass/Permit/Fees: It is free for residents to visit Lighthouse Point Park, but non-residents are charged $25 per vehicle, per day. There is also a $0.50 per person fee to ride the carousel.

Closest City or Town: New Haven, Connecticut

How to Get There: From Hartford: Take I-91 South for 38.8 miles to Main Street Anx in New Haven. Take Exit 50 to Townsend Avenue and travel 3.4 miles to the park's entrance.

GPS Coordinates: 41.1455° N, -72.5412° W

Did You Know? The Carousel at Lighthouse Point Park is one of the largest carousels ever built. It has 72 rideable figures mounted on 20 ranks and a 60-foot platform.

Yale Peabody Museum of Natural History

While the primary mission of the Yale Peabody Museum of Natural History is to support Yale University with geological, anthropological, and biological research, the museum is also designed to provide visitors with a record of the Earth's history through exhibits, publications, and educational programs. The museum has 10 permanent scientific collections that have enriched the community since 1866. *Fossil Fragments: The Riddle of Human Origins*, *Hall of Mammalian Evolution*, *Torosaurus: A Peabody Dinosaur*, *Daily Life in Ancient Egypt*, *Birds of Connecticut*, *Hall of Minerals*, and more are all open permanently to visitors.

Best Time to Visit: The hours are Tuesday through Saturday between the hours of 10:00 a.m. and 5:00 p.m., and on Sunday from 12:00 p.m. to 5:00 p.m.

Pass/Permit/Fees: There is no fee to visit the museum.

Closest City or Town: New Haven, Connecticut

How to Get There: From Hartford: Take I-91 South for 37 miles to Trumbull Street in New Haven, then take Exit 2 onto Bradley Street. Travel 0.4 miles to Whitney Avenue, where the museum is located.

GPS Coordinates: 41.3157° N, -72.9210° W

Did You Know? The earliest collection at Yale University was a "miscellaneous assortment of natural and artificial curiosities from around the world," which arrived at the university in the 18th century.

Yale University

Founded in 1701, Yale University is an Ivy League institution that serves to promote cultural understanding, discover more about the universe, improve the human condition, and train future world leaders. For more than 300 years, Yale has transformed education in the area from the establishment of a local college in 1640 to a world-class university in the 19th, 20th, and 21st centuries. It was named Yale in 1718 after Welsh merchant Elihu Yale, who donated 417 books, a portrait of King George I, and the profits from the sale of nine bales of goods to the school. Connecticut Hall, which was built in 1750, is currently the oldest structure in New Haven.

Best Time to Visit: If you want to visit during a less crowded time, choose the summer, when many students are away from campus. The fall is a perfect time to see the campus during the changing color of the foliage.

Pass/Permit/Fees: There is no fee to visit the Yale University campus.

Closest City or Town: New Haven, Connecticut

How to Get There: From Hartford: Take I-91 South for 37 miles to Trumbull Street in New Haven. Take Exit 3 onto Trumbull Street and travel for 0.1 miles to Yale University.

GPS Coordinates: 41.3163° N, -72.9223° W

Did You Know? Yale University became home to the first church contained within an American college when it established a Christian church in 1757. It is also home to the first literary review in the United States. *Yale Literary Magazine* was founded in 1836.

New Haven Green

Located in downtown New Haven, this 16-acre park is privately owned and often the site of festivals and other public events. The three 19th-century churches located within the park's boundaries have earned the park a National Historic Landmark District designation. New Haven Green has been a meeting place for New Haven residents since at least 1638, making it one of the oldest town greens in the U.S. At one time, it was the main burial location for New Haven residents, but in 1821, this practice ended, and the headstones were relocated to the Grove Street Cemetery. The bodies, though, were not moved, and between 4,000 and 5,000 people remain buried under New Haven Green today.

Best Time to Visit: The summer is when most festivals occur in the New Haven Green.

Pass/Permit/Fees: There is no fee to visit the New Haven Green, but there may be separate fees for festivals and other events.

Closest City or Town: New Haven, Connecticut

How to Get There: From Hartford: Take I-91 South for 37 miles to Trumbull Street in New Haven. Take Exit 3 onto Trumbull Street and drive 0.6 miles to Temple Street, where New Haven Green is located.

GPS Coordinates: 41.3082° N, -72.9261° W

Did You Know? New Haven Green was the parade grounds for the New Haven militia in the 1770s. Benedict Arnold led the militia, and it participated in the Battle of Bunker Hill during the American Revolution.

Kehler Liddell Gallery

This retail art gallery located in New Haven is operated by member artists with the intent to present, promote, and sell artwork from local contemporary artists. The Kehler Liddell Gallery was founded in 2003 by eight local artists in the Westville area of New Haven. It is now one of the longest-running retail galleries in the city. To become a member of the gallery, an artist must be juried, which means the operation of the gallery is conducted by a well-known group of accomplished artists.

Best Time to Visit: The gallery is open on Thursday and Friday from 11:00 a.m. to 4:00 p.m. and weekends from 10:00 a.m. to 4:00 p.m. It is open year round, and since it is indoors, it can be enjoyed at any time of year.

Pass/Permit/Fees: There is no fee to visit the Kehler Liddell Gallery, but the artwork and other items are for sale.

Closest City or Town: New Haven, Connecticut

How to Get There: From Hartford: Take I-91 South for 36.2 miles to Connecticut Highway 69 South/Whalley Avenue in New Haven. Take Exit 59, then drive 1.5 miles to Whalley Avenue, where the gallery is located.

GPS Coordinates: 41.3268° N, -72.9594° W

Did You Know? The 2,000 square feet of exhibition space in the Kehler Liddell Gallery make this the largest show space in the area. It can also be rented out for private events, where guests can mingle among the contemporary pieces.

The Blessed Michael McGivney Pilgrimage Center

Approximately 140 years of history of the Knights of Columbus are on display at the Blessed Michael McGivney Pilgrimage Center in New Haven. The Blessed Michael McGivney Pilgrimage Center was known as the Knights of Columbus Museum until it was renamed in 2020 in honor of the founder, Blessed Michael J. McGivney. The Knights of Columbus is the world's largest Catholic fraternal organization. It was established in 1882, and the museum opened in 1982 to celebrate the centennial of the organization. In addition to its permanent collection that chronicles the origins and growth of the Knights of Columbus, the museum also hosts temporary exhibits that feature religious art and history.

Best Time to Visit: The museum is open every day from 10:00 a.m. to 5:00 p.m., and because it is indoors, you can visit any time of year.

Pass/Permit/Fees: There is no fee to visit.

Closest City or Town: New Haven, Connecticut

How to Get There: From Hartford: Take I-91 South for 37.7 miles to Oak Street Connector in New Haven. Take Exit 1 and drive 0.6 miles to State Street, where the center is located.

GPS Coordinates: 41.30314° N, -72.92446° W

Did You Know? Father Michael J. McGivney founded the Knights of Columbus to foster unity, charity, and fraternity in local communities.

Beinecke Rare Book & Manuscript Library

This facility is one of the largest libraries in the world that is dedicated to preserving rare books and manuscripts. It is affiliated with Yale University and contains over 1 million books, several million manuscript pages, and tens of thousands of other objects like maps, photographs, paintings, and posters. While the main floor of the library is open to everyone, the research level is reserved for registered readers. The library's six-story glass-encased tower of book stacks holds about 180,000 volumes. Its name honors several Yale alumni donors: brothers Edwin J. Beinecke, Frederick W. Beinecke, and Walter Beinecke.

Best Time to Visit: The library is open Monday through Thursday from 9:00 a.m. to 7:00 p.m. and Friday from 9:00 a.m. to 5:00 p.m. It's a great place to visit at any time of year, but it may be less crowded in the summer or on school breaks.

Pass/Permit/Fees: There is no fee to visit.

Closest City or Town: New Haven, Connecticut

How to Get There: From Hartford: Take I-91 South for 37 miles to Orange Street in New Haven. Take Exit 3 onto Orange Street, then drive 0.5 miles to Grove Street, where you'll see the library.

GPS Coordinates: 41.3115° N, -72.9273° W

Did You Know? The library awards the Bollingen Prize for Poetry every two years and the Windham-Campbell Prizes every year.

Shore Line Trolley Museum

At Sprague Station, your journey on the Shore Line Trolley begins as you learn that the Shore Line Trolley is the "oldest continuously running suburban trolley line in the USA." In the museum, you'll discover more about the trolley history and the technology used throughout the years to operate the line. Then, you'll head outside, where you'll board a restored trolley car for a ride down Branford Electric Railway. Along the way, you'll see several restored trolleys in the museum's collection and enjoy the bucolic scenery of the countryside. You can bring a picnic to the museum's picnic grove and take as much time as you want to explore the grounds.

Best Time to Visit: Fall is the best time to visit for the most scenic trip down the trolley line.

Pass/Permit/Fees: Adult admission is $10, and children between the ages of 2 and 15 are $7. Seniors ages 62 years and older are $8, and children under 2 are free.

Closest City or Town: East Haven, Connecticut

How to Get There: From the north: Take I-91 South to I-95 North, then drive to Exit 51 or US-1. Turn right at the second light onto Hemingway Avenue (Route 142). Take the first left onto River Street, and the museum is on the left at the end of the street.

GPS Coordinates: 41.27507, -72.86291

Did You Know? The museum has a collection of nearly 100 vintage trolleys and has been open to the public since 1945.

Thimble Islands

Located in the harbor of Stony Creek, the Thimble Islands are an archipelago near the city of Branford. The islands consist of pink granite that used to be the tops of hills in the area before the last ice age. This granite foundation makes the Thimble Islands significantly more stable than other islands in the sound. The largest island is Horse Island, which measures 17 acres, but at least 22 others are inhabited, including Money Island (12 acres, 32 houses), Governor Island (10 acres, 14 houses), and Bear Island (home to a former granite quarry).

Best Time to Visit: Summer is the best time to visit the Thimble Islands because the boat trip is more pleasant in warm weather. Additionally, you should plan your visit for low tide to be able to see more of the islands.

Pass/Permit/Fees: There is no fee to visit the Thimble Islands, but you will need to pay for a boat ride to the islands.

Closest City or Town: Branford, Connecticut

How to Get There: From New Haven: Take I-95 East to Exit 56. Turn left at the light. Take the road to the next light, then turn left onto Leetes Island Road. Follow Leetes Island Road for 1 mile to the stop sign. Go straight as the road turns into Thimble Islands Road. Follow the road into Stony Creek and look for signs to the dock.

GPS Coordinates: 41.24713° N, -72.75715° W

Did You Know? The Thimble Islands, which were called *Kuttomquosh* ("the beautiful sea rocks") by the Mattabeseck Indians, are a waypoint for migrating seals.

Audubon Guilford Salt Meadow Sanctuary

The Audubon Guilford Salt Meadow Sanctuary consists of tidal wetlands that once spanned the entire Atlantic Coast from Georgia to Maine. There are many species of plants and animals that can only live in salt marsh conditions. This sanctuary also provides a nesting stop for various migratory birds. The exceedingly rare saltmarsh sparrow is one species that can only live in salt marshes, which are rapidly declining in number. You'll find one of the largest populations of saltmarsh sparrows in the world at the Guildford Salt Meadow Sanctuary.

Best Time to Visit: Spring and summer are the best times to visit the Audubon Guilford Salt Meadow Sanctuary to view some of the rarest species of animals and plants.

Pass/Permit/Fees: There is no fee to visit the Audubon Guilford Salt Meadow Sanctuary.

Closest City or Town: Guilford, Connecticut

How to Get There: From Hartford: Take I-91 South for 32.4 miles to Opening Hill Road in Madison. Take Opening Hill Road to the sanctuary's entrance.

GPS Coordinates: 41.30091° N, -72.64796° W

Did You Know? The 1-mile Anne Conover Nature Education Trail is appropriate for all hiking abilities. The trail is open daily from sunrise to sunset and allows visitors to see some of the rare bird and plant species that call the sanctuary home. Additionally, the sanctuary can be viewed by kayak or canoe from the East River.

Hammonasset State Park

This 2-mile beach is the largest shoreline park in Connecticut. There are also swimming facilities, campsites, and hiking trails, along with numerous activities like picnicking, scuba diving, saltwater fishing, and boating. Anglers enjoy this location for its abundance of winter flounder, summer flounder, weakfish, striped bass, bluefish, blackfish, and scup.

Best Time to Visit: The best time to visit Hammonasset State Park is between Memorial Day and Labor Day.

Pass/Permit/Fees: There is no fee for residents to visit Hammonasset State Park, but non-residents are charged $22 per vehicle on weekends and holidays, and $15 per vehicle on weekdays. The fee is reduced to $7 after 4:00 p.m. on all days.

Closest City or Town: Madison, Connecticut

How to Get There: From Hartford: Take I-91 South to Route 9 South. From Route 9, take Exit 9 and turn south onto Route 81. Follow Route 81 to I-95, then turn right. After 1 mile, take Exit 62 and turn left. Take Hammonasset connector for 1 mile and go through the light at Route 1 (Boston Post Road) to arrive at the park's entrance.

GPS Coordinates: 41.2667° N, -72.5578° W

Did You Know? The name *Hammonasset* is the Woodland Indian word for "where we dig holes in the ground," and the park's land used to be a farming area for Indians who lived along the Hammonasset River. The Winchester Repeating Arms Company owned the land between 1898 and 1920 as a testing site for its new rifle.

West Beach

This beach is the largest one in Westbrook and features spectacular views of Duck Island, Salt Island, and Menunketesuck Island. With a picnic area, a concession stand, a pier, and lifeguards, this beach doesn't offer as many amenities as other nearby beaches, but it's one of the best to visit if you're looking for a quiet day on the beach and in the water. West Beach is connected to Cummings Park by Cummings Marina, so if you're looking for more activities, you'll find ball fields, tennis courts, basketball courts, and beach volleyball courts just a short walk away.

Best Time to Visit: Summer is the best time to visit West Beach because the primary activity available here is swimming.

Pass/Permit/Fees: During July and August, there is a $25 parking fee for residents and a $40 parking fee for non-residents.

Closest City or Town: Westbrook, Connecticut

How to Get There: From Hartford: Take I-91 South for 35.5 miles to State Highway 621 in Essex. Take Exit 3 onto Connecticut Highway 153 and continue 6.6 miles to Seaside Avenue, where you'll see the beach's parking area.

GPS Coordinates: 41.2737° N, -72.4634° W

Did You Know? To avoid the parking fee, you can park your vehicle at Town Hall and walk approximately half a mile to the beach. If the beach parking lot is full, you can also park at Mulvey Municipal Center on weekends for a cost of $40 per vehicle.

Harvey's Beach

Harvey's Beach is one of the most popular beaches in Connecticut for boating, swimming, and fishing. It is approximately 100 yards long and is recognized for its fine white sand. The beach is open between Memorial Day and Labor Day for recreational activities. There are lifeguards on duty, a playground, a concession stand, restrooms, and a bath house. The beach area is fairly small until low tide, and most crowds will arrive after 12:00 noon because the beach expands after this time.

Best Time to Visit: Summer is the best time to visit Harvey's Beach, and while you can enjoy the beach before noon, it will be small in size until the tide goes out.

Pass/Permit/Fees: Parking is $10 per vehicle on weekdays and $20 per vehicle on weekends.

Closest City or Town: Old Saybrook, Connecticut

How to Get There: From Hartford: Take I-19 South for 1.2 miles from Whitehead Highway. Continue on I-91 South and Connecticut Highway 9 for 38 miles to 154/Middlesex Turnpike in Old Saybrook. Take Exit 2 onto Connecticut Highway 154 South. Follow Connecticut Highway 154 South, Boston Post Road, and Connecticut Highway 154 East for 4.2 miles to reach Toms Road and the beach.

GPS Coordinates: 41.27038° N, -72.39304° W

Did You Know? You'll want to use a tide chart app like Tides Near Me to determine when the tide is low at Harvey's Beach so that you go when the beach is at its largest.

General William Hart House

The home of General William Hart is a Revolutionary-era mansion that includes eight corner fireplaces, a historical garden, and authentic colonial décor. On the 45-minute tour, you'll be treated to such artifacts as Miss James's 1908 diploma from the Brooklyn School of Pharmacy, where she graduated as the only female in her class. The house was built in 1767, and the Harts had a reputation of often entertaining members of the community at their home with lavish parties. The General William Hart House is a perfect example of the type of home that affluent New England settlers lived in during the 16th and 17th centuries.

Best Time to Visit: The General William Hart House is only open by appointment, so contact the Old Saybrook Historical Society to book a tour.

Pass/Permit/Fees: There is a suggested donation of $5.

Closest City or Town: Old Saybrook, Connecticut

How to Get There: From Hartford: Take I-91 South for 38 miles to Connecticut Highway 154 South/Middlesex Turnpike in Old Saybrook. Take Exit 2 onto Connecticut 154 South and drive 2.6 miles to Main Street, where the house is located.

GPS Coordinates: 41.2872° N, -72.3749° W

Did You Know? From a second-floor bedroom window in his house, General Hart would have been able to see the Hart fleet of ships when they were in port and off the Hart dock at the North Cove entrance. This view would have aided his ability to lead the First Regiment of Connecticut Light Horse Militia.

The Preserve

This 963-acre forest, which spans three towns (Old Saybrook, Westbrook, and Essex), was considered the largest remaining unprotected forest on the coast between New York and Boston until it was acquired for conservation in 2015. A management plan for The Preserve is currently underway, which will create hiking trails and recreational opportunities in the future. Within The Preserve, visitors will find the Oyster River and tributaries of the Trout Brook and Mud rivers, all of which eventually find their way to the Long Island Sound. More than 25 amphibian and reptile species, 30 mammal species, and 57 bird species call The Preserve home.

Best Time to Visit: Spring is the best time to visit The Preserve to see much of the wildlife in the area.

Pass/Permit/Fees: There is no fee to visit The Preserve.

Closest City or Town: Old Saybrook, Westbrook, and Essex, Connecticut

How to Get There: From Hartford: Take I-91 South for 41.2 miles to Elm Street/Ingham Hill Road in Old Saybrook. Take Exit 67 onto Ingham Hill Road, then drive for 1.6 miles to Deer Run Road and The Preserve's entrance.

GPS Coordinates: 41.31667° N, -72.40818° W

Did You Know? The trails in The Preserve are not yet maintained or marked, but there are several hikes that will take visitors past wetlands, a scrub shrub swamp, an Atlantic white cedar swamp, and 38 vernal pools.

Katharine Hepburn Cultural Arts Center

Otherwise known as "The Kate," the Katharine Hepburn Cultural Arts Center's mission is to present a wide variety of performing arts to expose the citizens of Old Saybrook and Connecticut at large to meaningful educational and artistic opportunities. More than 20 performances a month are produced at The Kate, which means that guests are treated to 240 performances each year. Since its opening in 2009, The Kate has hosted over 1,500 performances, including ballet, music, dance, and even magic.

Best Time to Visit: There are performances at The Kate throughout the year, so the best time to visit depends on the type of performance you want to see. Consult the center's calendar on their website to choose a show.

Pass/Permit/Fees: There is no fee to visit the Katharine Hepburn Cultural Arts Center unless you see a show. The rates for each performance vary.

Closest City or Town: Old Saybrook, Connecticut

How to Get There: From I-95 North: Take Exit 67 from Connecticut Highway 154 West toward Old Saybrook. Merge onto Connecticut 154 West/Middlesex Turnpike, then take a slight left onto Main Street, where the center is located.

GPS Coordinates: 41.2904° N, -72.3755° W

Did You Know? In addition to the live performances at the center, The Kate has three satellite dishes that simulcast shows from the Bolshoi Ballet of Russia, the National Theatre of London, and the Metropolitan Opera.

Lynde Point Lighthouse

Also referred to as the Saybrook Inner Lighthouse, the Lynde Point Lighthouse is located on the west side of the Connecticut River on the Long Island Sound. Originally, there was a 35-foot wooden lighthouse in the area that was completed in 1803, but eventually, a new lighthouse was needed. In 1838, the funds to build the new lighthouse were secured, and the new 65-foot tower and six-room keeper's quarters were constructed. The lighthouse was continually improved through 1978, receiving a frame kitchen for the keeper's house in 1833, a duplex house in 1966, a fog bell in 1854, and another fog bell in 1883.

Best Time to Visit: Summer is the best time to visit Lynde Point Lighthouse.

Pass/Permit/Fees: The lighthouse can be viewed for free, but there is no public access to the lighthouse itself.

Closest City or Town: Old Saybrook, Connecticut

How to Get There: From Hartford: Take I-91 South for 38 miles to Connecticut Highway 154 South/Middlesex Turnpike in Old Saybrook. Take Exit 2 onto Connecticut 154 South and drive for 5.8 miles to Sequassen Avenue, where you'll see the lighthouse.

GPS Coordinates: 41.1617° N, -72.2036° W

Did You Know? The original lighthouse at Old Saybrook cost the Connecticut government $225 for the land and $2,200 for the construction of the wooden tower by New London carpenter Abisha Woodward. In 1838, the government appropriated a total of $7,500 for the new tower.

Connecticut River

Flowing for 406 miles, the Connecticut River is the longest river in New England. It travels through four states, starting at the U.S.–Canada border, and ends at the Long Island Sound. Some of the country's most fertile farmland is located in Connecticut around the river. During the 1600s, the river was either called *quinetucket*, a Mohegan word for "beside the long tidal river," or simply "The Great River." Puritans settled two large cities in the area that are still prominent today: Hartford and Springfield.

Best Time to Visit: The best time to visit the Connecticut River is in the fall when the foliage around the river is bursting with reds, oranges, yellows, and browns.

Pass/Permit/Fees: There is no fee to visit the Connecticut River.

Closest City or Town: Essex, Connecticut

How to Get There: From Essex: Take Railroad Avenue northwest toward Main Street/Middlesex Avenue. Turn right onto Middlesex, then left onto West Avenue. After 0.6 miles, take a right to stay on West Avenue, then turn right onto Main Street.

GPS Coordinates: 41.35184° N, -72.38481° W (These coordinates take you to the Connecticut River Museum located on the river.)

Did You Know? The first European explorer to sail the Connecticut River was Dutchman Adriaen Block, who sailed to Enfield Rapids in 1614. He dubbed the river the "Fresh River" and claimed it for the Netherlands.

White Sands Beach

If you're looking for spectacular views of Long Island Sound, White Sands Beach is an ideal location, with a gorgeous beach walk and access to Griswold Point Preserve. There is a section of beach that is open to the public, but it is surrounded by two private beaches, so be aware of the signs indicating when the public beach ends and the private beaches begin.

Best Time to Visit: Summer is the best time to visit White Sands Beach as the water will be warm enough to swim in.

Pass/Permit/Fees: There is no fee to visit White Sands Beach for residents, but a parking pass is required for visitors.

Closest City or Town: Old Lyme, Connecticut

How to Get There: From Hartford: Take I-91 South for 40.3 miles to Connecticut Highway 156 East in Old Lyme. Take Exit 70 onto Connecticut 156 and follow for 3.3 miles to Howard Road.

GPS Coordinates: 41.28043° N, -72.30454° W

Did You Know? Between June 16 and September 3, there are lifeguards on duty at this beach from 10:00 a.m. to 5:00 p.m. No alcohol is allowed on the beach; swim floats and rafts are also prohibited.

Florence Griswold Museum

The Florence Griswold Museum displays art from past and present, including notable works such as Childe Hassam's *Summer Evening (A Woman at the Window)* from 1886, John Ferguson Weir's *East Rock, New Haven* from 1901, and Matilda Browne's *Pionies* from 1907. The museum is housed in the former home of Florence Griswold, which was a haven for the Old Lyme Art Colony during the American Impressionism era.

Best Time to Visit: The Florence Griswold Museum is open Tuesday through Sunday between 10:00 a.m. and 5:00 p.m. (April through December) and Tuesday through Saturday between 10:00 a.m. and 5:00 p.m. (January through March). The gardens are in bloom during late spring and early summer.

Pass/Permit/Fees: Adult admission is $10. Students are $8 each, and seniors are $9 each. Children ages 12 and under are free.

Closest City or Town: Old Lyme, Connecticut

How to Get There: From Hartford: Take I-91 South to Route 9 South. Follow Route 9 to its end, then get back on I-91 going *north*. Go over the bridge at the Connecticut River and stay in the right lane. Take Exit 70 and turn left onto Route 156. At the second light, turn right onto Halls Road. Take Halls Road to its end, then turn left onto Lyme Street. The museum is the second building on the left.

GPS Coordinates: 41.32628° N, -72.32670° W

Did You Know? There are 12 acres of historic buildings, gardens, and hiking trails on the site.

The Robert and Nancy Krieble Gallery

The Robert and Nancy Krieble Gallery opened in 2020 as part of the Florence Griswold Museum. Four temporary art exhibits are showcased there each year. The gallery collaborates with renowned institutions such as the Portland Museum of Art, the Parrish Art Museum, and the Fenimore Art Museum to bring guests fabulous exhibits from all over the world. It overlooks the Lieutenant River and the spot where many boarders at Florence Griswold's home would set up their easels and paint the coastline.

Best Time to Visit: The gallery is open year round from Tuesday through Sunday between the hours of 10:00 a.m. and 5:00 p.m. (April through December), and Tuesday through Saturday between the hours of 10:00 a.m. and 5:00 p.m. (January through March).

Pass/Permit/Fees: Adult admission is $10. Students are $8 each, and seniors are $9 each. Children ages 12 and under are free.

Closest City or Town: Old Lyme, Connecticut

How to Get There: From Hartford: Take I-91 South to Route 9 South. Follow Route 9 to its end, then get back on I-91 going *north*. Take Exit 70 and turn left onto Route 156. At the second light, turn right onto Halls Road. Take Halls Road to its end, then turn left onto Lyme Street. The museum is the second building on the left.

GPS Coordinates: 41.32631° N, -72.32675° W

Did You Know? Nancy Brayton Krieble was a local philanthropist who had a passion for American art. She donated more than $4 million to local art facilities.

Rocky Neck State Park

Rocky Neck State Park is one of the best options for families, as it has a diverse trail system for all abilities, a soft-sand beach, picnic areas, birdwatching platforms, and more. You can even try your hand at crabbing or fishing, or take some time to watch the trains go by. The clear waters off the beach make it a perfect swimming hole, and the picturesque salt marsh is a wonderful backdrop for photos. At 710 acres in size, this park has something for everyone, and it is one of the most popular recreational areas in the state.

Best Time to Visit: Summer is the best time to visit Rocky Neck State Park for warm-water swimming and camping, which runs from May through September.

Pass/Permit/Fees: There is no fee for residents to visit Rocky Neck State Park, but non-residents will be charged $22 per vehicle on weekends and holidays, and $15 per vehicle for weekdays. After 4:00 p.m., the fee for non-residents is $7.

Closest City or Town: Niantic, Connecticut

How to Get There: Take I-95 to Exit 72 and follow the turnpike connector south to Route 156. Turn left onto Route 156 and travel 0.25 miles to the park's entrance.

GPS Coordinates: 41.3170° N, -72.2413° W

Did You Know? There are numerous historic sites throughout the park, including the stone Ellie Mitchell Pavilion on the western shore. The building was constructed in the 1930s out of wood cut from every state park and state forest.

Ocean Beach Park

With sugar-fine white sand, Ocean Beach Park is one of the most popular recreational beaches in Connecticut. Not only do you have excellent access to the Atlantic Ocean, but you can also swim in an Olympic-size freshwater swimming pool. There's also an 18-hole miniature golf course, a banquet and conference facility, the Boardwalk Café Food Court, a spray park, amusement rides, a game room, a nature walk, a health club, and a playground on the property.

Best Time to Visit: The park is only open between Memorial Day and Labor Day.

Pass/Permit/Fees: Parking is $20 on weekdays and $25 on weekends and holidays, except for July 4, when the fee is raised to $35. A discounted price of $15 is available after 6:00 p.m. Pedestrians are $8 each.

Closest City or Town: New London, Connecticut

How to Get There: From Hartford: Take Bob Steele Street and Columbus Boulevard to Connecticut Highway 2 East. For 32 miles, follow Connecticut 2 and Connecticut 11 to Connecticut 82 East in Salem. Take Exit 4 onto Connecticut 85 South and Ocean Avenue to reach the park's entrance.

GPS Coordinates: 41.30928° N, -72.09928° W

Did You Know? Ocean Beach Park hosts numerous special events throughout its open season.

Bluff Point State Park

If you're looking for a place where you can really get away from the city and take time to connect with nature, Bluff Point State Park is the place to go. It's the last remaining piece of undeveloped land on the coast of Connecticut. There is a wooded peninsula that extends out on the Long Island Sound. It measures just 1.5 miles long by 1 mile wide. The bluff is only accessible by foot or non-motorized vehicle, and it passes through a wooded area before opening wide to the water.

Best Time to Visit: It is best to visit Bluff Point State Park between April and October.

Pass/Permit/Fees: There is no fee for residents to visit Bluff Point State Park, but non-residents are $15 per vehicle on the weekends and holidays, and $10 per vehicle on weekdays.

Closest City or Town: Groton, Connecticut

How to Get There: From the north: Take Exit 88 from I-95 North and turn right onto State Road 117 South. At the end, turn right onto Route 1 South. Turn left at the first light onto Depot Road and follow it to the park's entrance.

GPS Coordinates: 41.33571° N, -72.0333° W

Did You Know? The bluff is the remnant of a time when glaciers covered the entire state. When they melted approximately 17,500 years ago, the waters of the Long Island Sound eroded the bluffs, forming the beach below. This is a process that is ongoing, and you'll find that sometimes the beach is colored red or black, while other times it is white.

Mystic River and Village

The Mystic River is an estuary located in the southeast corner of Connecticut that empties into the Fishers Island Sound and divides the towns of Stonington and Groton in Mystic Village. At one time, there were three shipbuilding companies located on the Mystic River, and you can retrace this history at the Mystic Seaport Museum that is now in their place.

Best Time to Visit: Spring and fall are the best times to visit Mystic River when the heat is not at its summer peak.

Pass/Permit/Fees: There is no fee to visit Mystic River.

Closest City or Town: Mystic Village, Connecticut

How to Get There: From Harford: Take State Street 0.2 miles to Connecticut Highway 2 East. Follow Connecticut Highway 2 East and Connecticut Highway 11 South for 32.0 miles to Connecticut Highway 82 East. Take Exit 4 and get on I-95 North. Drive for 11.7 miles to Connecticut Highway 27-North/Greenmanville Ave. Take Exit 90 and follow Connecticut Highway 27 to Fair Acres Circle.

GPS Coordinates: 41.36526° N, -71.98830° W (These coordinates will take you directly to the Mystic Seaport Museum!)

Did You Know? The Mystic River gets its name from the Pequot word *missi-tuk*, which describes a river that experiences waves that are driven by wind or tides. The Pequot Indians lived along the western bank of the Mystic River in a village called Siccanemos until it was destroyed during the Pequot War in 1637. This is known as the Mystic massacre.

Hopeville Pond

There are 544 acres at Hopeville Pond State Park. The Pachaug River, which runs through the park, has been a major fishing location dating back to when the land belonged to the Mohegan Indians. When the water is low, you can still see the stone weirs that the tribes built to direct water flow to the center of the stream, where they were trapped by baskets. Anglers flock to the park to catch northern pike, catfish, yellow perch, largemouth bass, smallmouth bass, chain pickerel, and bluegill.

Best Time to Visit: If you plan to stay the night at the park, the best time to visit is mid-April to September 30.

Pass/Permit/Fees: Hopeville Pond is free to visit for residents, but non-residents are $15 per vehicle on weekends and holidays, and $10 per vehicle on weekdays.

Closest City or Town: Griswold, Connecticut

How to Get There: From I-395: Take Exit 24. If coming from the north, turn left. If coming from the south, turn right. Follow Hopeville Road and the signs to the park. When you get to the Y intersection, bear right. Travel 0.5 miles to the park's entrance.

GPS Coordinates: 41.60515° N, -71.92664° W

Did You Know? In colonial days, a sawmill and cornmill were constructed on the Pachaug River, where there used to be natural waterfalls. (They are now underwater.) In 1818, the sawmill and cornmill were joined by another sawmill, a woolen mill, a gristmill, and a satinet mill named Hope Mill.

Millers Pond

Millers Pond is a unique body of water in Connecticut due to the fact that its main source comes from underground springs that create a pond of unpolluted water. This means it's an excellent habitat for smallmouth bass and trout. There has been a dam on the pond since at least 1704, and likely prior to that. It was built by Thomas Miller to create a reservoir that would provide water for his gristmill downstream. There is no beach or boat launch at the pond, and it's principally a quiet, scenic location rather than a place for recreation. There is a 1.5-mile hiking trail in the park that is ideal for all skill levels.

Best Time to Visit: While the scenery at the pond is gorgeous all year long, the best time to hike the trail is between April and September.

Pass/Permit/Fees: There is no fee to visit Millers Pond.

Closest City or Town: Haddam, Connecticut

How to Get There: From Route 9: Take Exit 11 and follow Route 155 West. Turn left onto Millbrook Road, then take a slight left onto Foothills Road. You will see the parking area on the right.

GPS Coordinates: 41.48081° N, -72.63214° W (These coordinates will take you directly to the parking lot.)

Did You Know? Within Millers Pond State Park's boundaries, there are approximately 5 miles of trails, but it has access to at least 11 miles of additional trails, including one that will take you to the Bear Rock overlook. Swimming is prohibited in the pond, but fishing is allowed.

Devil's Hopyard State Park

Chapman Falls, a waterfall that drops over 60 feet, is the main attraction in Devil's Hopyard State Park, an 860-acre park located near East Haddam. The waterfall was once the power source for Beebe's Mills from the 1700s until 1890. Devil's Hopyard. The hike to Vista Point Cliff gives visitors a spectacular view of Eightmile River. Several bridges in the park are on the National Register of Historic Places.

Best Time to Visit: If you're a fisherman or swimmer, spring and summer are the best times to visit.

Pass/Permit/Fees: There is no fee to visit.

Closest City or Town: East Haddam, Connecticut

How to Get There: From Connecticut Route 9: Take Exit 7, then turn left onto Connecticut Route 82 East/154 North. Turn right at the first light and follow the signs to the park's entrance.

GPS Coordinates: 41.48484° N, -72.34218° W (These coordinates will take you to the Chapman Falls parking lot.)

Did You Know? Before erosion and river formations were well understood, early settlers believed the potholes near the falls were created by the Devil when his tail accidentally got wet as he was passing by. He became angry and burned the holes in the rock with his hooves when he ran away. The potholes are perfectly cylindrical and are made by stones that were trapped in an eddy and spun around, wearing depressions in the rock.

Cockaponset State Forest

Cockaponset State Forest is the second-largest state forest in Connecticut and provides numerous recreational opportunities for visitors, including hunting, fishing, hiking, mountain biking, horseback riding, boating, snowmobiling, and cross-country skiing. While swimming is typically allowed in the area, the inland beaches are closed at times. Please check state websites for current information on access. The forest covers 17,000 acres of land, a portion of which (Chester Cedar Swamp) has been declared a National Natural Landmark. This swamp is a prime example of an Atlantic white cedar forest and is at risk of being overtaken by hemlock trees.

Best Time to Visit: The forest has activities for all seasons, but the fall is the most popular time to visit for the foliage.

Pass/Permit/Fees: There is no fee for residents to visit Cockaponset State Forest, but non-residents are charged $15 per vehicle on weekends and holidays, and $10 per vehicle on weekdays.

Closest City or Town: Haddam, Connecticut

How to Get There:
From Middletown: Take Route 9 South to Exit 6. Turn right onto Route 148 and travel west for about 2 miles. Turn right onto Cedar Lake Road and go another 2 miles. You'll see a sign for Pattaconk Lake, where you'll turn left into the forest's entrance.

GPS Coordinates: 41.4598° N, -72.5208° W

Did You Know? The Cockaponset State Forest is named for an Indian chief who is buried in Haddam.

Gillette Castle Park

William Hooker Gillette, a relatively famous director, playwright, and actor, built his castle atop the most southernly point of the Seven Sisters hill chain. However, it only looks like a castle on the outside. Inside, you'll discover a 24-room mansion with 47 doors, no two of which are exactly the same. The mansion's furnishings are all built in and include a movable table on tracks. On the grounds, there is a private 3-mile-long narrow-gauge railroad that belonged to Gillette and numerous hiking trails that feature stone arch bridges, wooded trestles, and near-vertical steps.

Best Time to Visit: While the castle is only open to tours from Memorial Day to Labor Day, the best time to see it is during the holidays when the castle is decorated.

Pass/Permit/Fees: There is no fee to visit the Gillette Castle State Park, but the tour is priced at $6 for adults and $2 for children ages 6 to 13. Children ages 5 and under are free.

Closest City or Town: East Haddam, Connecticut

How to Get There: From I-91 South: Take Exit 22 onto Route 9, then drive to Exit 7, a bridge crossing the Connecticut River. Follow the signs to the park's entrance.

GPS Coordinates: 41.4230° N, -72.4284° W

Did You Know? William Hooker Gillette was the son of U.S. Senator Francis Gillette and Elizabeth Daggett Hooker Gillette, but his parents did not support his pursuit of acting. His quirky castle was his retirement home beginning in 1910.

Goodspeed Opera House

Home to Goodspeed Musicals, the Goodspeed Opera House was constructed in 1877 by William Goodspeed, a local banker and merchant. However, its intended purpose was never to present operas, but to showcase live theater, such as *Charles II*, the first play to show at the house in October 1877. When William Goodspeed died, the plays were halted. It was later used as a militia base during World War I and a general store. In 1959, a group of citizens formed Goodspeed Musicals to save the building after the state of Connecticut condemned the structure. The group raised funds to restore the building and maintain it. Eventually, it reopened in 1967 for musical productions.

Best Time to Visit: The musical season runs from April to December, but tours are available on the fourth Saturday of each month between May and October.

Pass/Permit/Fees: A tour of the Goodspeed Opera House is $5 for adults and $1 for children between the ages of 6 and 12. Children under the age of 6 are free. Musical rates vary based on performance and date.

Closest City or Town: East Haddam, Connecticut

How to Get There:
From Hartford: Take I-91 South to Exit 22 South. Go south on Route 9 to Exit 7. At the end of the ramp, turn left, then turn right at the first stoplight. The theater is on the right side just over the bridge.

GPS Coordinates: 41.4518° N, -72.4625° W

Did You Know? Since 1968, Goodspeed Musicals has produced more than 250 musicals.

Wadsworth Falls State Park

Mountain Laurel, Big Wadsworth, and Little Falls are the main attractions at Wadsworth State Park. You can also enjoy swimming in a freshwater pond or relaxing on 300 feet of beach. There are plenty of hiking trails that are suitable for all ages throughout the park. Wadsworth Falls drops 30 feet into the Coginchaug River, and you can take a 1.5-mile easy hike to a nearby viewpoint. Little Falls has a longer drop of 40 feet, but less water flows over the fall. The park is 285 acres in size and features numerous picturesque views.

Best Time to Visit: In spring, the waterfalls will run fuller and faster.

Pass/Permit/Fees: There is no fee for residents to visit Wadsworth Falls State Park, but non-residents will be charged $15 per vehicle on weekends and holidays. On weekdays, there is no fee for any visitor.

Closest City or Town: Middletown, Connecticut

How to Get There: From Hartford: Take I-91 South to Route 9 South, then take Route 9 South to Middletown. Take Exit 15 to Route 66 and stay on this road through Middletown. Watch for the signs to the park and turn left onto Route 157. You will see the park's entrance on the left.

GPS Coordinates: 41.53742° N, -72.68604° W

Did You Know? The park is named for Clarence C. Wadsworth, a scholar, linguist, and National Guard colonel who wanted to preserve the area for the public to enjoy.

Dinosaur State Park

At Dinosaur State Park, you'll find one of the largest dinosaur track sites in the U.S. and Canada. You can observe fossil tracks from the early Jurassic period and explore over 2 miles of hiking trails that feature more than 250 plant species, including conifers, magnolias, ginkgoes, and more. Many of these plants were around when dinosaurs still walked the earth. In addition to the natural features in this park, you can also visit the museum and the geodesic dome exhibit. Along the trails, you'll even see broken basaltic rocks that were part of a volcano that flowed over the dinosaurs' land.

Best Time to Visit: Spring is the best time to visit Dinosaur State Park.

Pass/Permit/Fees: Adults are $13 each, and children between the ages of 6 and 12 are $2 each. Children ages 5 and under are free.

Closest City or Town: Rocky Hill, Connecticut

How to Get There: From Hartford: Take I-91 South to State Highway 411/West Street. Take Exit 23 onto State Highway 411/West Street, then continue 1 mile to the park's entrance

GPS Coordinates: 41.6519° N, -72.6569° W

Did You Know? Scientists believe the Dilophosaurus was responsible for making most of the tracks in Dinosaur State Park. This large carnivorous dinosaur first appeared in the early Jurassic period and is believed to be the first meat-eating dinosaur of this size. Eubrontes tracks are also found in the park.

Proper Planning

With this guide, you are well on your way to properly planning a marvelous adventure. When you plan your travels, you should become familiar with the area, save any maps to your phone for access without internet, and bring plenty of water—especially during summer months. Depending on the adventure you choose, you will also want to bring snacks and even a lunch. For younger children, you should do your research and find destinations that best suits the needs of your family. Additionally, you should also plan when to get gas, local lodgings and where to get food after you're finished. We've done our best to group these destinations based on nearby towns and cities to help make planning easier.

Dangerous Wildlife

There are several dangerous animals and insects you may encounter while hiking. With a good dose of caution and awareness, you can explore safely. Here is what you can do to keep yourself and your loved ones safe from dangerous flora and fauna while exploring:

- Keep to the established trails.
- Do not look under rocks, leaves, or sticks.
- Keep hands and feet out of small crawl spaces, bushes, covered areas, or crevices.
- Wear long sleeves and pants to keep arms and legs protected.
- Keep your distance should you encounter any dangerous wildlife or plants.

Limited Cell Service

Do not rely on cell service for navigation or emergencies. Always have a map with you and let someone know where you are and for how long you intend to be gone, just in case.

First Aid Information

Always travel with a first aid kit with you in case of emergencies. Here are items to be certain to include in your primary first aid kit:

- Nitrile gloves
- Blister care products
- Band-aids - multiple sizes and waterproof type
- Ace wrap and athletic tape
- Alcohol wipes and antibiotic ointment
- Irrigation syringe
- Tweezers, nail clippers, trauma shears, safety pins
- Small Ziplock bags for containing contaminated trash

It is recommended to also keep a secondary first aid kit, especially when hiking, for more serious injuries or medical emergencies. Items in this should include:

- Blood clotting sponges
- Sterile gauze pads
- Trauma pads
- Second-skin/burn treatment
- Triangular bandages/sling
- Butterfly strips
- Tincture of benzoin
- Medications (ibuprofen, acetaminophen, antihistamine, aspirin, etc.)
- Thermometer
- CPR mask

- Wilderness medicine handbook
- Antivenin

There is so much more to explore, but this is a great start.

For information on all national parks, visit: www.nps.gov.

This site will give you information on up-to-date entrance fees and how to purchase a park pass for unlimited access to national and state parks. These sites will also introduce you to all of the trails of each park.

Always check before you travel to destinations to make sure there are no closures. Some hikes close when there is heavy rain or snow in the area, and other parks close parts of their land for the migration of wildlife. Attractions may change their hours or temporarily shut down for various reasons. Check the websites for the most up to date information.

Printed in Great Britain
by Amazon